BONNIE AND CLYDE

Discover More of History's Worst

Adolf Hitler

Jack the Ripper

—HISTORY'S WORST—
BONNIE AND CLYDE

BY JAMES BUCKLEY JR.

Aladdin

New York   London   Toronto   Sydney   New Delhi

ALADDIN

An imprint of Simon & Schuster Children's Publishing Division

1230 Avenue of the Americas, New York, New York 10020

First Aladdin hardcover edition April 2018

For information about special discounts for bulk purchases, please contact Simon & Schuster
Special Sales at 1-866-506-1949 or business@simonandschuster.com.

The Simon & Schuster Speakers Bureau can bring authors to your live event.
For more information or to book an event contact the Simon & Schuster Speakers Bureau
at 1-866-248-3049 or visit our website at www.simonspeakers.com.

Designed by Nina Simoneaux

The text of this book was set in Adobe Caslon Pro.

Manufactured in the United States of America 0318 FFG

2 4 6 8 10 9 7 5 3 1

Library of Congress Cataloging-in-Publication Data

Names: Buckley, James Jr., author.

Title: Bonnie and Clyde / James Buckley.

Other titles: Bonnie & Clyde

Description: New York : Aladdin, 2018. | Series: History's worst | Audience: Age: 8-12. |
Includes bibliographical references and index.

Identifiers: LCCN 2017005121 (print) | LCCN 2017035248 (eBook) |
ISBN 9781481495509 (eBook) | ISBN 9781481495493 (hc) | ISBN 9781481495486 (pbk)

Subjects: LCSH: Parker, Bonnie 1910-1934—Juvenile literature. |
Barrow, Clyde, 1909-1934—Juvenile literature. |
Criminals—United States—Biography—Juvenile literature. |
BISAC: JUVENILE NONFICTION / Biography & Autobiography / Historical. |
JUVENILE NONFICTION / History / United States / 20th Century. |
JUVENILE NONFICTION / Law & Crime.

Classification: LCC HV6245 (eBook) | LCC HV6245 .B78 2018 (print) |
DDC 364.15/52092273—dc23

LC record available at https://lccn.loc.gov/2017005121

CONTENTS

INTRODUCTION

No Bonnie . . . no Bonnie and Clyde.

Without Bonnie Parker, Clyde Barrow would probably still have been a criminal and a murderer . . . but he wouldn't have been famous.

No Bonnie . . . no book, no movie, no romance.

Without blond and perky Bonnie Parker, the story of Barrow and his gang of thugs would be one of hundreds of crime stories that dotted the twentieth century, but it would not have become the romantic tale of tragic love that people know it as today. A woman's involvement in crime, especially violent crime, was a novelty, then and now, and Bonnie's role in the story set it apart from other tales of death and flying bullets.

No Bonnie . . . no pictures . . . no story.

There were lots of other villains in the 1930s when Bonnie and Clyde were rambling around the Midwest killing people. But few, if any, of those villains provided the viewing public with such memorable snapshots of themselves. Thanks to a cache of photos found in 1933 and splashed around the newspapers of the world, Bonnie and Clyde were the first nationally known criminals to have a face beyond a mug shot. By actually seeing these outlaws as real people and not just invisible stories on the radio, the general public had faces to see and remember. Bonnie and Clyde were the first criminal media superstars, but without Bonnie in the pictures, Clyde would have been back-page news.

THE STORY OF the short and deadly life of the girl with big dreams and the boy from dirt-poor Dallas is filled with tragedy and blood and death. But their story is larger than that.

Bonnie and Clyde did their deadly deeds in a time that saw the rise of mass media that spread the celebrity culture that we continue to live in today. (I'm talking to you, reality shows!)

Their "adventures" came at a time when Americans were starving to death from lack of food, but found some relief in the exploits of "bad guys" (and a girl, in this case). Their story exposes the horrible realities of the Depression, when banks became the people's enemy and anyone who seemed to be opposing banks suddenly was cheered from the sidelines.

Their story is also about how we track and attack crime and criminals as a society. Today, we take for granted that law enforcement can go anywhere and do anything (within the law) to keep us safe. Until the era of Bonnie and Clyde (and other headline-grabbing killers of the time), that was not the case. Crime, it turned out, helped create the engines of its own destruction.

Throughout this story of Bonnie and Clyde, you'll see how these strands weave together. A terrible poverty of both money and spirit that leads to antisocial and criminal choices . . . the coincidence of an increase in media just when a story like theirs came along . . . the need among people for heroes, even if those heroes turn out to be murderers . . . the way that people of all genders are fascinated when a woman "goes bad" . . . the way the forces of law and order came to change and how Bonnie and Clyde showed them how.

Add in fast cars, photography, newsreels, Hollywood stars, advanced weapons, gangland slang, colorful lawmen, jailhouse poetry, and J. Edgar Hoover, and you've got a perfect script for a crazy tale. The only trouble? That story left widows and orphans and heartbroken parents in its wake.

So, yes, Bonnie and Clyde get their own book, but it's not a guidebook. It's a tale of tragedy.

ROMANTICIZE

There's a word, or a concept, that you should understand to truly "get" the story of Bonnie and Clyde. You've heard of romance. Valentines and hearts and flowers and love songs and proposals—romance. But there's a related word: *romanticize* (roh-MAN-tih-size). It means to make something that is not that pleasant, good, or remarkable into something that is all those things. It means to put a positive spin on issues or events

4

that were probably not that positive. So when people look back "fondly" at the story of Bonnie and Clyde, they sometimes choose the love story of the two villains and ignore the pain they caused. People "romanticize" stories like this one, and that feeling is important to understand when trying to figure out why killers get so much attention.

Sometimes romanticizing can be sort of innocent. You might look back at a time in your life when things were mostly hard, but there were some good times—so you focus on those. People who grew up in poverty but have escaped might remember the close family times, and not the moments of hunger or want. On the other hand, romanticizing can also hide the truth. Even as the Barrow gang's car races through a starry Texas night and a loving couple shares exciting moments and cozy riverside camping—and romance—the reasons they are speeding away and the death they left behind cannot and should not be forgotten.

1

BUD

This story starts in Texas. Now, that's a big place, so to narrow it down, take a drive south along a road from the big city of Dallas to a tiny little bit of nothing called Telico. It's very small now and was even smaller then, just around the turn of the twentieth century.

Henry and Cumie Barrow, a young couple in love, had married in 1890 and decided to take up farming, as so many did in the wide-open spaces there. In their first years they began to raise crops such as cotton and corn. When the farm did not produce, Mr. Henry Barrow hired himself out to work on other folks' farms. His wife, Cumie, sixteen when they married, ran the house, which, in the way of things back then, was soon filled with kids.

Cumie was just nineteen and married three years when the couple's first child, Elvin, came along in 1894. In the decade that followed, the Barrows had two more sons and a daughter.

It was a hard life, but manageable for the most part.

One of the stars of this story, Clyde Barrow, came along on March 24, 1910. At least that's what it said in the Barrow family Bible, which to a Texas family was more official and reputable than anything from a government office. There were no doctors around to fill in any paperwork—a midwife was on hand, but that was about it. Most reports say he was born in 1909, but later researchers have never been able to turn up anything official for either date. (The FBI added their own bit of myth, calling him Clyde Champion Barrow on its Wanted posters. Clyde's family, including sister Nell, said his middle name was Chestnut.)[1]

Two more kids followed in the now very crowded Barrow household. Among the five Barrow siblings, the second-most notable was Ivan, known by one and all as Buck. Clyde got a nickname of his own: Bud. Together, Buck and Bud would become partners in crime and constant companions.

By the time of Clyde's arrival, the Barrow family all lived in a three-room house (most histories call it a "shack"[2]). There was no running water and no electricity. This was not unusual, even in the early 1900s. Electricity didn't really arrive in most rural areas for decades. The bright lights of the big city of Dallas, however, shone in the far distance, both literally and figuratively.

The children were not at all interested in becoming farmers like their parents. But Cumie worked hard to make them go to school and to do chores around the farm. With such a large group of siblings (the seventh and last Barrow child, Marie, was born when Clyde was almost eight), finding people to play with was no problem. Nearby farm families provided other playmates for the young Barrows.

Cumie also was a devout Christian. She believed that one should do everything that Jesus and the Bible and her church said to do. And when the kids didn't do what either Jesus or Cumie said, she was ready with a switch. She aimed at their legs most often.

The children also spent chunks of time visiting or even living with their uncle, Frank Barrow, Henry's brother. He lived on a larger farm in Corsicana, Texas.

A DOUBLE HIT TO FARMERS

The early 1920s were very difficult for farmers in Texas and across the Midwest.

The first reason was economic. World War I had ended in late 1918. During the war, prices for most farm crops such as wheat, corn, or cotton had risen dramatically. The government was buying a lot and that kept prices high. Farmers were doing well generally. However, once the war ended, those prices fell quickly. By 1920 and 1921 many farmers were struggling to make ends meet.

In Texas in particular, another reason was environmental. A beetle called the boll weevil had infested the cotton crop there. It destroyed acres and acres of farms, ruining some farmers. The effects of the weevil spread throughout towns that depended on cotton, and many families were left in poverty.

The Barrow family's farming fortunes would soon turn, too, in part for these reasons.

———————————————————————————————

Clyde had it pretty good in Telico, for all its shortcomings. He had friends and plenty to do. He went to school but never did that well, nor did he seem to care much one way or the other. Buck, Clyde's older brother, stopped going to school when he was about eight. Like their father, he never really did learn to read or write.

Clyde had work to do on the farm, but it left him time for fun, such as riding the calves or playing cowboys and Indians.

He didn't seem particularly aimed for a criminal life. A story told by his sister Marie years later was a rare example. It seems that the candy store owner caught Clyde trying to walk out with a handful of sweets. To prevent the youngster from eating any evidence of future crimes, the owner "made Clyde whistle every time he came into the store."[3] It was hard to whistle with a mouth full of swiped candy.

His sister Nell reported that her older brother once almost

11

drowned in a river. "He was perfectly limp by the time we got him on the bank," she wrote.[4] But he revived and together they promised to hide the incident from their parents, so they would not forbid them further swimming adventures.

But those were rare dramatic incidents in a seemingly quiet life.

Things would soon change.

By the time Clyde was about thirteen, most of his older siblings had moved up and out to Dallas to make their way in the world. Due to falling crop prices and the increasing lack of family help, the Barrows found that running the farm was becoming harder and harder. Henry had found part-time work in a brickyard, but it was not enough. They made the hard decision to move. Henry and Cumie upped stakes with their three youngest kids and left their small farm. Next stop: the big city, or at least near enough to one.

2

LITTLE BONNIE

Meanwhile, a little girl named Bonnie Parker was growing up in west Texas with big dreams. Like the Barrows, the Parker family lived in a small farming town, Rowena. Unlike the Barrows, the Parkers did not depend on farming. Instead, Charles Parker was a brick mason. That is, he built things such as houses, sheds, and walls using bricks and cement. For his wife, Emma, this gave her family a slightly higher social standing in the little town. And like Cumie Barrow,

Emma made sure her family was a big part of the local church, the First Baptist.

On October 1, 1910, Bonnie Parker was born, joining two-year-old brother, Hubert, known as Buster. (The family added a second daughter, Billie Jean, three years later.) By the time she was three, Bonnie was singing in the church. On one occasion, however, Bonnie departed from the script and sang a country-music tune instead of a hymn. As many biographers since have interpreted this, "She'd wanted extra attention, and she got it."[5]

It's important to point out that most of what we know about Bonnie's early life is from one major source: her mother. In 1937, Emma contributed an account of her daughter's life to a book called *Fugitives*. Clyde's sister Nell contributed part of the other half of the Bonnie and Clyde story in the same book.

The stories Emma told of Bonnie and Clyde's life of crime are easily backed up by news accounts and witnesses. The stories she told about her daughter's early life are less easily proven. Most historians have had to take her at her word. Was every story of young Bonnie absolutely true? Perhaps not all of them, and that adds to the romantic history of this tale. By matching up stories from her young life that showed what she later became, was Emma (or co-author Jan Fortune) adding to the mythology? Or trying to explain what had happened to her baby girl?

Whatever her motives, Emma's stories filled in gaps in Bonnie's history. For example, there was the time that a visiting uncle taught Bonnie some swear words. Such talk was quickly forbidden by her strict parents, but the story fits with the rough-and-tumble life Bonnie later led.

Some stories are more easily backed by facts. The 1914 death of Charles Parker is one such fact, and it played a huge role in the family's life. As a result, Emma had to leave Rowena and move back near her parents. The Parker widow and her children settled in Cement City, near Dallas. Emma found work as a seamstress and the family all lived with her parents in a suddenly crowded house.

Bess Krause was Bonnie's cousin. In the *Fugitives* book, she told author Fortune about life in Cement City. Bess talked about Bonnie's reluctance to do what she was told. One story was that Bonnie cut off a bag of smelly herbs called asafetida sometimes worn around the neck by the girls. The belief was that the smells would ward off colds and flu, but mostly they just smelled terrible. Bonnie the rebel was having no part of this stinky ritual.

The factory-filled and dirty Cement City was a far cry from farmlike Rowena. Emma hated it there but tried to make the best of it. She continued to make the children go to church, though now each visit involved a miles-long walk on dusty or muddy roads.

Stories about Bonnie's somewhat rowdy young life continued. She once found and drank enough of the wine her grandfather had hidden to pass out. She apparently liked to light fires, though nothing too large. (She and Bess did start one fire near a barn that they had to douse quickly with buckets of water before it spread.) And she had a problem with keeping her cool, taking part in fights at school with both boys and girls. "She was always in a scrap of some sort," her mother wrote.[6] But Bonnie did like to have attention paid to her. One story that Emma tells is about a school performance. In those days, white (and sometimes black) theater performers would put on heavy makeup called "blackface" to supposedly make themselves look like Africans. They would then sing songs connected with what was considered the African or African-American slave culture. At one such event Bonnie was in makeup but had her wig pulled off suddenly. Her bright blond curls made quite a contrast with the dark black face paint and the audience pointed and laughed. According to Emma, the young Bonnie was not embarrassed, but instead took the opportunity of being in the spotlight to do some gymnastic moves, which got the audience on her side.

Bonnie had her eyes on the future, and those eyes had stars in them. She wanted to be a Broadway star, singing and dancing and enjoying wide fame. She learned popular songs and broke them out at family dinners. She even tried writing poetry, a hobby she would continue for some time.

Her role models in her quest for fame were the people she saw in movie magazines. The 1920s had brought in the "flapper" look, which combined short hair, short dresses, and long strings of pearls. Tiny hats completed the outfit, and Bonnie and her friends tried to dress the part, even though it was hard given their lack of money.

From her earliest days in school, her relatives said, there were always a lot of "fellers."[7] While Bonnie relished the attention—and the candy and treats that boys gave her—she was always clear who was the boss of any relationship. Bess wrote that Bonnie once threatened one boy with a razor blade for making her mad. Bess wrote that "when Bonnie loved, she loved with all her heart."[8]

When Bonnie was fifteen, she finally found a boy she could stick with.

3

BUD AND BUCK

From a snug if less-than-perfect farmhouse, five members of the Barrow family moved to Dallas to seek a better way forward. What they found at first was little more than a tent. They could not afford a house or rooms, so they joined numerous other arriving farm families in campgrounds. The families, such as the Barrows, slowly moved from tents into homemade shanties built from scrap lumber. Cooking and washing were done outside. Food could be hard to come by, but generous

Dallas residents sometimes sent bread out to the camps to help.

To make what little money was available, Henry worked as a peddler. He basically gathered junk from all over town in a wagon and drove around trying to sell it. The family had brought a horse with them from the farm to help with such jobs. But it was hard going, and the family struggled.

They got a little help from their four older children, who had moved to Dallas before their parents and the younger kids did. Daughter Nell and daughter-in-law Drusilla worked at a beauty parlor and sent some money. An older son, Jack, was a car mechanic. He sometimes hosted the family at his house, which he shared with a wife and the first of what would eventually be his four children.

A few years after arriving in West Dallas, Henry finally saved up enough money to open a store. It actually included a gas station for the cars that were quickly replacing the horses in the area. Automobiles had only been produced for wide use since the early 1910s, and they were still far from the "everyone's got one" state of the world today.

Meanwhile, Buck's life was not as stable as his siblings. He had not found a job that would settle him down, and he moved often. He sold chickens for a time, but also kept dogs with which he tried to win money in fights with other people's dogs. He also did some peddling, but instead of finding junk to sell, he stole it. He was the first Barrow to be arrested after the police caught him with a load of stolen metal.

Buck was married, too, and had twins, though one died as an infant. This did not seem to stop him from seeking out trouble, however. In time, younger brother Clyde gravitated to his older brother. He regularly started skipping school to romp with a roving pack of young teenagers. The calm life on the Telico farm was far behind him as he saw the fun—legal and illegal—to be had in the wild streets and alleys of the big city.

He wasn't all bad. Clyde's sister Marie later wrote that her older brother loved music. He tried out several instruments, though never stuck with one for very long. His sister Nell told a story about the two of them combining their money to buy a ukulele, which they learned to play together. Nell's husband played the saxophone, and Clyde would sometimes give that a try too.

Cumie also thought she still could influence Clyde. When

he was fourteen, he was baptized in an official church ceremony. This is a key step in the life of a Christian. In some non-Catholic Christian faiths, baptism is not performed on infants but on older people who make the choice to do so themselves. Of course the question as to whether Clyde chose to do so out of belief or because he loved his mother might be answered by his later path in life.

But the allure of a life like Buck's was too much. In 1926, when Clyde was sixteen, he dropped out of school for good. To bring in the money that he wanted to buy nice clothes—by this time, his interest in the opposite sex was clear—he went to work. He worked for a company that baked crackers, then for a factory, then at a glass company. There, he learned to install windows and work with glass. Marie remembered the family keeping a mirror that Clyde had made. He later worked at a pie company and a paint shop. He never liked the work and always had an eye out for another way to bring in the money he wanted. Buck helped by teaching Clyde how to hot-wire cars. A new kind of electric starter had recently been invented for automobiles. It made starting cars easier than the hand-crank that older cars used. But it also made stealing cars easier, and Clyde soon made this a big part of his criminal routine.

When he was seventeen, Clyde was dating a woman named Eleanor Williams (though Nell said the young woman's name was Anne), and he wanted to take her for a spin. He was able to rent a car, but he didn't let the car company know that he planned to take a trip outside of town. When the time for return came and went, the company contacted the police. The Barrows explained that Clyde and Eleanor had gone to a nearby town. When police arrived at the address, Clyde bolted. After returning to Dallas shortly thereafter, he was arrested. The car was returned and Clyde was released, but it was the first step on the short but active connection between Clyde Barrow and the police. (About this time, he also showed some of the shortsightedness of youth. He had Eleanor's name tattooed on his arm. After they broke up, he added his next girlfriend's name, Gladys, who was not happy to share space with the previous girl.)

His second "brush with the law"[9] came in early 1927. Buck had obtained a truckload of turkeys—and in this case "obtained" means almost certainly stolen. The pair was caught by sheriff's deputies, and though Clyde was let go—Buck took the fall for his brother—it began a period of brotherly crime. Some stories Clyde later told described a string of burglaries. Buck himself was arrested in 1928 for car theft, but later got off. (The Barrow family made the trip to San Antonio, the site of Buck's trial, in the horse-and-wagon. Henry picked cotton at farms along the way to earn traveling money.) Also, by early 1929 Buck had left his wife for Blanche Caldwell, whom he would later marry and who would join the brothers on future criminal adventures.

During this period in West Dallas, Clyde met other people who would remain a part of his life. W. D. Jones was another boy about his age. The two young men stayed in touch, and Jones later played a big part in the Barrow gang. He also had a friend named Clarence Clay. Several years later Clarence's sister married a man who also had a sister—a woman who would change Clyde's life forever.

4

TEENAGE BONNIE

For her part, Bonnie was heading into some life-changing moments as well. By the time she was fifteen, her early cuteness had turned into head-turning beauty. She was described as being very small—less than five feet, and a hundred pounds—but with memorable blue eyes and bright blond hair. Her love of performance gave her an air of confidence, while her take-no-prisoners style put up a challenge to any possible suitors.

One young man, however, made it through her gauntlet. Roy

Thornton had left high school a few years earlier, though he was only a couple of years older than Bonnie's fifteen. She fell for him in a big way, and over the objections of her mother, she decided to marry him. In a foreshadowing of her later permanent love, Bonnie had a pair of hearts and the words "Bonnie and Roy" tattooed on her leg. They were married on September 25, 1926.

But for all of Bonnie's wishes for an amazing romance—inspired by the movies she watched with friends and the breathless magazine stories they read—the reality of marriage did not match up with her dreams. For one thing, she didn't want to leave her mother, which is not surprising since Bonnie would have been a high school sophomore at this point, were she still going to school. She and Roy got a house near her mother's place, but Bonnie spent most of her time with her mother. Emma described being carried by Roy during a bad rainstorm from the couple's house back to her own home. Within a few weeks, after daily visits between mother and daughter, the married couple moved back in with Emma.

Roy, it was soon apparent, was not exactly a perfect husband. He didn't seem to work very much, but always seemed to have money. In the summer of 1927 he went away and did not return for ten days. He never said where he'd gone or why. He did similar vanishing acts again in October and December. In between he drank often, and some accounts say that he hit Bonnie.

Bonnie, picking up on her young love of writing and poetry, kept a diary for a short time. At the beginning of 1928 she wrote, "I wish to tell you that I have a roaming husband with a roaming mind. We are separated for the third and last time. I love him very much . . . but I am not going to take him back."[10]

By the middle of January, Roy had not come back, so Bonnie was forced to take a job as a waitress. She spent a year working and living with Emma, with no word from Roy.

Roy returned in early 1929, but Bonnie, as she had written, did not take him back. He was in jail soon after, serving five years for robbery. Bonnie remained married to Roy for the rest of her short life, however.

She continued working as a waitress, at one point almost losing her job for giving away meals to people who could not pay. One customer later wrote that Bonnie told him that she wanted to be a "singer or maybe a poet."[11]

It seemed that the dreams she had for stardom and/or Hollywood romance faded, though she continued watching the movies that fascinated and inspired her.

She wrote more than once in her short diary entries, "Why don't something happen?"[12]

She would not have to wait long.

~ **5** ~

A CRASH

While Bonnie and Clyde were living their young lives and starting on the roads that would soon connect them, America was taking a detour off its own road to success. In the 1920s, the period known as the Roaring Twenties, many Americans had lived pretty well—Dallas slums and West Texas excepted, among other places. Companies took risks and borrowed too much money in the hope of turning it into even more money. Banks loaned out more money than they really had in hopes of taking advantage of the rise in stock prices. The prices on the stock market rose and rose. Meanwhile, agriculture continued to struggle. The value placed on many things—homes, businesses, land—was far too high. Something had to give.

In late 1929 everything changed for America. On October 29, 1929, known as Black Tuesday, the stock market in New York City crashed. It was not like an auto crash, but its effects were nearly as devastating. Stock prices plummeted in a day. The value of millions of people's life savings evaporated. Almost overnight, thousands of businesses were suddenly facing closure. Banks closed by the thousands because too many desperate people wanted to withdraw all their money at once . . . and the banks simply didn't have it.

The stock market crash was the beginning of the Great Depression. For most of the next decade, Americans struggled mightily just to survive. Millions of people lost their homes and were forced to take to the road. Thousands more lived in tent cities called "Hoovervilles" after the president (until early 1933), Henry Hoover. Soup kitchen lines were common in major cities, mostly in the Northeast. Unemployment rates neared 30 percent.

Not until the US government under President Franklin Roosevelt, elected in 1932, started numerous programs to revive the economy did things start looking up. And the impact of those programs was not really felt until the mid-1930s.

It's important to know about the Depression because it was the black cloud under which America lived during the time that Bonnie and Clyde and other outlaws gained their fame. Because of the way that the crash had kick-started the bad economic times, Americans looked on banks and large businesses as the enemy. They felt that the bankers and stock speculators had led America into ruin, taken the people's money, and broken laws. The organizations that had once been trusted and looked up to were suddenly the villains.

So when outlaws began to stick up banks or rob from businesses, people saw a bit of payback. They saw people doing something about their trouble instead of waiting in a soup line or scrounging for food to feed their children. They wondered if they themselves could have the guts to take the risks that the outlaws were taking. Most of those outlaws were men, but when the female villain Bonnie Parker was suddenly thrust into the public eye, women imagined they could be her and men wished they could meet her.

The Depression certainly didn't "cause" Bonnie and Clyde, but it gave them a ready-made stage on which to act.

Down in Texas the Depression was not quite as noticeable as in the big cities up north. The farm-based economy in the state had already been reeling from post–World War I troubles. But the Depression surely didn't help, and money was even more short than usual, from the downtown banks to the struggling farmers.

Clyde Barrow didn't worry about his next job. He knew where the money was and he knew what he had to do to get it.

6

A FATEFUL MEETING

By late 1929 Clyde was regularly committing crimes with a changing group of partners, including Buck. Most crimes were theft, of cars or goods from stores. Other times they broke into houses and stole jewelry and any cash they found.

Around Thanksgiving that year, about a month after Black Tuesday, the group's activities finally led to real trouble. Very early one morning in Denton, Texas, they stole a small safe from a car mechanic's garage. They figured they could take the safe someplace ... safe ... and crack it at their leisure. Police saw the car speeding away from the garage and tried to pull them over to investigate. At the wheel, Clyde floored it and raced away.

The chase went on for several miles, but Clyde eventually crashed their car. As the Barrow boys tried to run, the police opened fire and Buck was hit in the legs. Clyde escaped after hiding under a nearby house.

Once again Buck took the fall. He never ratted out his brother. He was convicted of the robbery and was sentenced to four years in prison. He had recently met Blanche Caldwell, the woman who would become his Bonnie; though she was herself married, she told Buck she'd wait for him to get out of prison and then be his forever.

Clyde was sorry to see his brother go away for a stretch, but soon things were looking up.

THE JANUARY 5, 1930, meeting between Clyde Barrow and Bonnie Parker has been romanticized to death.

On that evening Clyde's old pal Clarence Clay invited Clyde to join him when he visited some friends. Buster Parker was married to Clarence's sister, and Buster had also invited his sister, Bonnie.

In a house on Herbert Street in Dallas, Bonnie met Clyde. And the rest is history.

Bonnie was out of work, having lost her waitress job when the restaurant closed in the wake of the economic downturn. Clyde was mostly committing crimes, but was lying low as the police were looking for him.

It was, as the stories all say, love at first sight. Clyde was single. Bonnie was still officially married to Roy, but long separated. The pair found in each other exactly what they were looking for. To Bonnie, Clyde was a confident, well-dressed, successful man. Even his success in less-than-legal ways appealed to her, adding a bit of danger to the situation. He had a nice car and she thought immediately they could have some fine adventures.

For his part, Clyde saw a bubbly, blond, fun-loving young woman who was not at all put off by his choice of lifestyle. Bonnie wrote later that she admired his "dark wavy hair and dancing brown eyes."[13]

Buster Parker, Bonnie's brother, was later quoted as saying, "You could see the sparks fly between them."[14]

In the years since, in movies and documentaries, this moment in their lives has been dramatized and romanticized. Even people who were there each tell slightly different stories. In some, Bonnie was there to help a friend with a broken arm, giving her a bit of mercy to balance the later crimes. In some stories Bonnie doesn't know about Clyde's past. In others she's thrilled to meet someone with a checkered history.

However it happened, though, the record of the next month or so is clear. They went everywhere together. Movies, dinners, drives in the country—it was the stuff of Bonnie's romantic dreams.

But in February the romance hit a roadblock. While visiting Bonnie at Emma Parker's house, Clyde was arrested for a series of crimes he had committed in previous weeks and months. Though only "with" Clyde for a month, Bonnie went wild when he was taken away. She pulled on the police officers who came for Clyde, trying to get them away from her man. One report says that she pounded the walls of her house in frustration.

Clyde was put in jail in Dallas, where Bonnie began a series of regular visits while he awaited trial, just like the romantic heroines of the movies she loved. She wrote him letters, in one even telling him about another man who had courted her and brought her candy. "I didn't appreciate the old candy at all," she wrote. "And I thought [instead] about my old darling in that mean old jail."[15] In another letter, after hearing that he had been sent for trial for the safe robbery with Buck—police easily connected the criminal brothers—she wrote, "I was so blue and mad and discouraged, I just had to cry. I laid my head down on the steering wheel and sure did boohoo."[16]

Her romantic streak showed in yet another letter. "They only think you are mean I know you are not and I'm going to be the very one to show you that this outside world is a swell place, and we are young and should be happy like other boys and girls instead of being like we are."[17]

She had known Clyde a month, but she was completely committed. It is this devotion that became one of the driving forces of this story and of many people's attraction to Bonnie.

7

BONNIE'S IN THE GANG

As it turned out, Clyde did not face any punishment for his role in the safe robbery. However, even as he was let go for that, he was arrested again for crimes he had committed in nearby Waco, Texas. They included car theft and robbery, seven counts in all. After a short trial in March 1930, Clyde was convicted and sent to prison for the first time. He received seven two-year sentences, but was allowed to serve them all at once.

Bonnie immediately promised to wait for him. Clyde had other ideas.

He knew that he would soon be moved to a harsher prison in Huntsville, Texas, from the county lockup in Waco. Clyde had big plans in the world and did not want to spend any time under lock and key if he could help it. He looked around at his situation and came up with a plan. To succeed, he would need Bonnie's help.

She visited him often in jail, and during one of those visits, he told her where he knew a gun was hidden in the home of one of his partners in crime. He wanted Bonnie to get the gun and smuggle it in to the jail. While it was one thing for Bonnie to wait for her man loyally and patiently, this was another step. He was testing her devotion to him and making her, for the first time, an accomplice to his crimes.

She passed the test. He gave her a note with a map of the partner's house. On the map he wrote "You are the sweetest baby in the world to me. I love you," under the drawing.[18]

Bonnie found the gun and returned to the jail with the weapon strapped under her dress. There was no search of visitors in those days, certainly not of the sweet, devoted girlfriend who had become a daily sight to the guards. Clyde got the gun and got to work.

A few days later, Clyde and two fellow prisoners lured a guard to their cell. They showed him the gun and forced him to release them. They locked the guard in the cell and ran past another on duty at the door. That second guard chased them and fired off several shots, but all missed. The convicts were away into the Waco night.

Clyde stole one car, then a better one as they made their getaway. The swap helped fool the police, and they kept switching cars over the coming hours.

Back in Waco the breakout was front-page news. Bonnie saw that the plan had worked but had not heard from Clyde. She left Waco for Dallas and waited nervously for several days. She finally got a telegram from Clyde from a town in Illinois. Clyde and his partners had made their way there, stealing cars or money as needed to keep moving.

Their trip was cut short in Middletown, Ohio. After they tried to rob a railroad station, they were later chased by police when their stolen car was spotted. They actually made the mistake of driving back by the station after getting away cleanly. Their error led the Waco papers to label the criminals "dumbbells."[19] The two fugitives were caught quickly. Clyde raced away but could not elude the police in the car he had stolen. It was a lesson he would remember in the future—steal better cars.

Though he tried to pretend he was someone else, Clyde was quickly identified as the escaped Texas outlaw. Back in Waco, the newspaper read BABY THUGS CAPTURED,[20] a nod to the youth of Clyde.

Clyde appeared before the same judge who had let him serve his seven prison terms at the same time. Clyde was not as lucky this time. "You keep breaking into houses, and some of these days you're going to either get shot or shoot somebody else," the judge said, foreshadowing, of course, Clyde's deadly future.[21] He then sentenced Clyde to serve all seven terms one after the other, a fourteen-year stretch. Unless something happened, Clyde would be in his midthirties before he tasted freedom again.

His brother Buck was luckier. In the same month that Clyde was on the run, Buck was on the run too, having stolen a guard's car and escaped from prison in Huntsville. He would remain free for nearly a year.

After a month in the county jail, Clyde was sent to Huntsville Prison. Upon entry, he lied and said he was eighteen, not twenty. He made up a new middle name, Champion, for some reason. He also wrote that Bonnie was his wife. This was not true, but it meant that the prison would pass on letters that she wrote.

In one she wrote, "If you have to go down, I'll be good while you're gone, and be waiting—waiting—waiting—for you. I love you."[22] The love that would define their lives was clearly already firmly in place, at least in Bonnie's eyes.

He was sent to several other cities in the coming months to face other charges for crimes ranging from murder to car theft. He was not convicted of any, and once all the legal paperwork was finished, he was finally assigned to what was supposed to be his long-time home: Eastham Farm in Houston County, Texas.

His transportation to the farm was known as the One-Way Wagon. That is, anyone who rode in it was probably not coming back. The wagon was a truck with a metal box on the back. Prisoners were placed inside it on benches and then had chains fastened around their necks. On the bouncing ride on dirt roads in brutal Texas heat, it was a terrible way to travel. On the wagon Clyde met another inmate named Ray Fults who had some experience at Eastham, as he had escaped from there a year earlier and was now being taken back.

The meeting with Fults and the ensuing time at Eastham would prove to be a life-changing experience for Clyde.

8

CLYDE IN PRISON

Clyde Barrow had lived in some very unpleasant places. The shack the Barrow family shared in the Dallas slums was cold, dirty, and drafty. He had crashed in rooming houses during his time on the run. He'd camped out during other flights from the law. But those were all palaces compared to Eastham Farm.

In those days the point of prison was to punish criminals, not to rehabilitate them. Prisoners were not there to learn a trade and reform before returning to society. They were in prison to face brutal punishment in payment to society for whatever they had done. The men slept in large rooms filled with bunk beds. The showers rarely worked, and the toilets stood out in the open at the end of the dorm buildings. If the prisoners acted up, guards could fire bullets in from the windows, aiming high to scare the prisoners ... or low, to do more damage. Outside, piles of garbage attracted rats.

Inmates were used as work gangs, fed little more than bread and water, and watched by gun-toting guards on horseback. The prisoners were rarely allowed to clean themselves and wore uncomfortable scratchy wool jumpsuits. In fact, in Texas they were little more than slave labor. Local farms or factories could pay the prison to have the men, chained together to prevent escape, come and work. When they were not on farms, some of which were owned by the prison, the inmates were given menial tasks such as breaking rocks, digging ditches, or helping maintain railroad tracks. It was hot, hard, brutal, painful, and awful.

If prisoners objected to any of this treatment, they could be beaten. One punishment was known as "riding the barrel."[23] A prisoner was handcuffed and placed atop a pickle barrel. He had to stand there for hours, slowly becoming tired and cramped. If he fell, he was disobeying again and would be beaten or put back on the barrel. A prisoner who escaped and was caught would be beaten with sticks and gun butts in front of the other prisoners as a warning. Clyde's sister Nell later wrote that she visited him and saw him with two black eyes, and that he had told her a story of watching one prisoner knife another to death.[24]

Another form of punishment at Eastham was known as "the bat."[25] It was a leather strap on a wooden handle, and guards used it to beat the backs and legs of prisoners. All the other prisoners had to watch this bloody spectacle. According to author Jeff Guinn, sometimes during the beatings, "sand would be poured into the victim's open wounds."[26]

Ray Fults later worked with author John Neal Phillips to write a long story about his life. Fults's account is the basis for most of the stories about life in Huntsville with Clyde. In the book Fults told of being brutally beaten after he was returned following an escape. Guards pistol-whipped him so that his face was swollen and bleeding badly. Clyde tried to make the guards stop and was nearly beaten for his trouble. But, according to Phillips, "Fults was impressed with Barrow's show of loyalty."[27] Fults also said that Clyde promised him that one day they would be out of there and would come back and free their fellow prisoners.

It was not just the guards that were brutal. Other prisoners, bigger and stronger, took advantage of the smaller, younger inmates. In Clyde's case, his nemesis was a man named Ed Crowder, in prison for robbery, but whose repeated escape attempts and prison violence had extended his sentence to ninety-nine years. Crowder was never leaving Eastham. Because of his size and physical power, Crowder had been given the job by the guards of being the inmate in charge of the dorm Clyde lived in. Crowder was allowed to enforce his own rules inside, helping the guards by keeping the inmates in line while guards watched from outside. Crowder was a brute. He saw in Clyde a small, young inmate, and soon he was beating Clyde regularly. He also began sexually abusing Clyde. This brutality went on for months, and there was little that Clyde could do to stop it.

Then Clyde got some help. An older inmate named Aubrey

Scalley, who was already sentenced to life in this awful place, came to Clyde with an idea. If Clyde wanted to do something about Crowder, this other inmate would say he did it. That is, Clyde might be able to get away with getting rid of Crowder. To this point, other than fighting other inmates and trying to fight off Crowder, Clyde had not used violence. He stole money or stole cars, but he didn't use a gun and he didn't beat his victims. But now he would need to make a fateful choice or face Crowder throughout his long time at Eastham.

With Scalley's encouragement, Clyde came up with a plan. He managed to find a length of metal pipe during his work in the fields and hid it in his clothes. On the evening of October 29, 1931, Clyde Barrow became a murderer, and not for the last time. This first time, he lured Crowder into the shower area and bashed in his head with the pipe. Scalley then came in and put on a show, stabbing Crowder's lifeless body with a sharpened stake. When the guards came in, they found a bloody Scalley standing over the dead Crowder. The hulking Crowder was buried in the crowded cemetery on the prison grounds. Scalley remained in prison (he was later cleared of the murder after pleading self-defense). Clyde was free of torment.

But he was still in prison. And as of late 1931, so was Buck. Clyde's older brother had been free since escaping Eastham more than a year earlier. But his wife Blanche convinced him that he'd never truly be free until he finished his time. So he turned himself in and went back to the Farm.

Clyde did not have his brother's resolve. Even with the death of Crowder, he still faced an awful existence, so he made another awful decision. Whether he did it himself or got someone else involved is not known for sure (his sister Nell says it was another convict, not Clyde himself[28]), but what is known is that Clyde ended up losing the big toe and one other on his left foot. By being so injured, went his plan, he would be spared some of the most unpleasant work on the Farm.

To his shock, he was let out of Eastham just weeks later, on February 2, 1932. His mother and other family members had been petitioning the governor to let him out, and they'd finally succeeded.

The nearly two years he'd spent at Eastham had hardened Clyde. His previous criminal life was centered around cars and robbery and spending money on nice clothes, and at least for a while, on Bonnie. From this point on, crime would continue to be his career, but he would approach it with a deadly ferocity. Fults later wrote that because of prison, Clyde changed "from a schoolboy to a rattlesnake."[29]

For his part, Clyde told his parents, "I'm not going back to the hellhole. They'll have to kill me first."[30]

THE FIRST BARROW GANG

When Clyde returned from prison, one of his first moves was to find Bonnie. In the latter stages of his time away, her letters had slowed to a trickle. She had been getting on with her life, even having another boyfriend for a time. But he was still stuck on her—and she on him—and wanted her back in his life for good. For her part, she was overjoyed when he showed up, on crutches due to his injured foot, jumping into his arms in front of her new beau and crying out,

"Darling!"[31] Though Emma Parker tried to stop it, Bonnie and Clyde were together again. They would only rarely be apart until the day they died.

Clyde made some tentative attempts to go straight, as the saying goes. He worked with his dad at the gas station Henry had opened the year before. He was also hired and fired from a series of jobs away from the station. He even tried moving to Framingham, Massachusetts, to work with a friend of his mother's, but he was lonely for Bonnie and was soon back in Dallas. He was also regularly hassled by the police. They knew his criminal history and would often bring him in for questioning about a crime or just to let him know they were watching him. Before Eastham, Clyde would probably have chalked this up to part of the deal for a life of crime. Afterward, however, it continued the process of him becoming a full-time criminal. The police were just another form of prison guard putting him in his place, using intimidation instead of violence, but still making Clyde feel small and powerless.

In this unsettled time, Ray Fults arrived in Dallas. He, too, had been pardoned from Eastham, but had jumped right back into crime. He actually showed up at Henry's station in a stolen car to connect with Clyde.

Together, Fults and Clyde and another partner, Raymond Hamilton, formed the first version of what would come to be called the Barrow gang. Bonnie was, of course, invited along for the ride and came willingly. This was the life of excitement she had dreamed of. This was the daring move that a film star would make, not the choice of a lonely Dallas waitress. She had been thrilled by her part in the Waco jail break and wanted to see what else awaited her.

For the next several months, in the first part of 1932, the Barrow gang pulled off a series of robberies with varying levels of success. They broke into an oil company office only to find the safe empty. In Minnesota they robbed a bank of $33,000. In that incident Fults waved a pistol and a shotgun while Clyde leaped over a counter and forced the bank manager to open the vault and give them bags of cash. They added robberies and thefts of various sizes as they traveled from state to state. This method of moving around often helped them stay more than one step ahead of the law. At this time law enforcement was on a local level only.

Police in one town or county usually could not arrest or even follow criminals to another town or county, and certainly not from state to state. By the time they contacted their fellow state police elsewhere, the criminals were long gone and the trails cold.

INTERSTATE HIGHWAYS

The roads for the Barrow gang were literally paved by the federal government. After World War I, the Federal Highway Act was passed to make a system of roads for the cars that were being bought by the tens of thousands. Before cars, roads were mostly dirt and traveled by horse and wagon. Cars needed smoother roads to run well, so hundreds of thousands of miles were paved with asphalt or concrete. Maps were made that showed these routes around the nation, and the gang made regular use of them to find escape roads.

One of the main goals for Clyde and Fults was their dream of breaking back into Eastham and rescuing the men left behind there. They knew they would need more men and more guns—

and even bulletproof vests—so much of their criminal activity was aimed at raising funds for that mission. It would take them more than two years to finally make it happen. For his part, Hamilton didn't want to be part of any such raid and left them after a robbery in Illinois that netted the gang a stash of powerful guns.

With Eastham still on their minds, the gang's crime spree continued. They ranged through nearly a dozen states, stealing cars as they needed them. Clyde preferred the powerful Ford V-8, a new car with the biggest engine yet made. Most police departments didn't have cars anywhere near as fast, so he could easily speed away from any pursuit. Clyde also developed into an outstanding driver, skilled and daring.

In April in Amarillo, Texas, their stolen car let them down, its engine sputtering out. As they walked back to town, police arrived to check out what seemed to be three drifters. Instead, the cops found themselves facing Clyde's .45 pistol. A moment later, another member of the growing gang, now called the Lake Dallas gang, showed up with a working stolen car. The group kidnapped the three policemen, adding a new crime to their tally.

The kidnapping ended soon after when the outlaws let the

officers loose, but the chase continued after they commandeered a mail carrier's car. The carrier, named Bill Owens, would later be able to tell the tale of being in the car while the gang raced from the police. At one point Clyde smashed through a toll road barrier at the border between Texas and Oklahoma. Gunshots followed them into Oklahoma. Clyde heard on the radio about upcoming roadblocks, so he let Owens (and his mailbag) go. The mailman then made an odd request: Would Clyde burn the car instead of abandoning it? Owens wanted the post office to buy him a newer, nicer car. In the first of many signs that Clyde liked people and simply hated cops, he and the gang burned Owens's Ford to the ground the next day. They escaped the pursuit and returned to Dallas.

The plan to go into Eastham remained uppermost in their minds, and their next move was designed to prepare the men inside the camp for the raid. They brought Bonnie along to help, as she could enter the prison as a guest. She met with Clyde's old savior, Aubrey Scalley, and let him know what was coming. He should get things ready inside the camp for the big day.

Their next move was to get cars big enough to carry away the freed inmates. They found them in Tyler, Texas, and then drove to nearby Kaufman to rob a gun store they had seen earlier. It did not go well. Almost as soon as they stopped the big cars, they were spotted by a night watchman. He fired at them and they returned fire, and then they leaped back into their cars. The town fire bell went off, alerting everyone to the action. It was a chase.

In their big, powerful cars and with experience in high-speed driving, Clyde and Fults quickly gained ground. But then they ran into a roadblock—two huge road grading machines blocked the highway. The cars raced back through Kaufman, where yet another roadblock had been put up. A dirt road off the main highway seemed to be another way out, so both cars rumbled onto it. A sudden rainstorm—and it can rain suddenly and hard in Texas—turned the dirt road into a tire-sucking mud path.

The trio had to abandon the cars and try to run through the fields, shoes sticking with every step. They reached a farmhouse and stole the only thing on hand—mules. Fults rode one and Bonnie and Clyde rode another. They rode the stolen animals until they reached a home with a car, which they stole and drove until it ran out of gas. That's when their pursuers finally caught up to them.

~ 10 ~

BONNIE'S JAIL STINT

onnie, Clyde, and Fults had been keeping ahead of a growing crowd of lawmen and townspeople for hours. The mules had taken them first, then the car, but now their luck had run out. The trio raced into the woods, hoping to find shelter. They dove into a shallow ditch as the first of their pursuers neared. A gunfight broke out, as farmers, police, and others fired rifles and shotguns at the trio. Clyde and Fults fired back with pistols; Bonnie helped reload the weapons.

As the people firing at them closed in, Fults was hit in the arm and began bleeding badly. At this point Clyde knew they could not all escape. As Fults described it, Clyde shouted that he'd come back for them and vaulted out of the ditch. He ran past two of the surprised policemen and disappeared into the darkness. A few moments later Fults was out of ammo and was captured. Bonnie gave herself up as well.

In the tiny jail, a doctor was called to tend to Fults's arm wound. The medical man turned out to be the owner of the car the trio had stolen after their mule ride, and he refused to work on the thief's arm.

Fults was finally treated the next day and was transferred to another prison to face new charges of kidnapping from an earlier incident. Bonnie remained in jail. She was visited by Blanche and other Barrow family members. Emma remembered this time as one that broke her heart, even more so because she was too poor at the time to help her daughter.[32] Marie Barrow reported that Bonnie "was glad to see us and didn't seem to have the slightest bit of bitterness against Clyde or our family."[33]

While she spent three months in prison, Bonnie had plenty

of time on her hands. She returned to her former hobby of writing poetry. She collected them together under the heading "Poetry from Life's Other Side." The most famous of the poems she wrote in jail was called "The Story of Suicide Sal." It was filled with slang words and terms used by gangsters, both in real life and in the movies Bonnie loved watching. The poem included terms like "moll," "joint," "inside job," "the rap," and "henchmen," among others. The growing crowd of well-known criminals (see page 83) was dominating headlines, and Hollywood was making movies dramatizing this lifestyle. Bonnie was paying attention. The end of the poem read,

Not long ago I read in the paper

That a gal on the East Side got "hot,"

And when the smoke finally retreated,

Two of gangdom were found "on the spot."

It related the colorful story

Of a "jilted gangster gal."

Two days later, a "sub-gun" ended

The story of "Suicide Sal."

In June, Bonnie's case was finally heard in court. She stuck with the story that she and Fults had come up with—that she was in fact a kidnap victim hauled along by the pair of thieves. Partly because of that and partly because few people believed that a woman would ever be involved in such crimes, Bonnie was released without charge on June 17.

Her mother, Emma, thought that perhaps Bonnie had put Clyde behind her. Emma wrote that Bonnie had said as much and had then taken a job in Dallas so she could live with Emma again. But it was not true. Bonnie had continued to see Clyde every time he returned to Dallas in the summer of 1932. Emma came to realize that Bonnie "loved him so madly, so insanely and so without rhyme or reason that she would have stayed with him anyway, no matter what came."[34]

Meanwhile, back in Dallas, Clyde, who had left Bonnie behind to be arrested, continued his criminal ways. Clyde believed that he was gathering guns and money in what he hoped would be an attempt to break Bonnie out of jail. It turned out that he didn't need to, but it fueled his decisions all that spring.

He robbed an oil company office and some other stores and

gas stations. On April 30, for the first time, he took part in a crime that resulted in someone's death. Clyde was the getaway driver when some partners robbed a jewelry store. The owner, Joseph Bucher, was shot and killed after he opened the safe for the men. Unfortunately for Clyde, Bucher's wife had recognized him from a visit to "case the joint," as the robbers say. Because he was part of the crime, Clyde was a murderer in the eyes of Texas law. They would never stop chasing him.

The hunt for Clyde grew over the summer. The Texas governor put out a reward for his capture and wanted posters went up around the state. As the stories in the newspapers about Clyde's crimes piled up, according to Nell Barrow, reports often said that witnesses saw a blond woman waiting at the car while Clyde carried out the crimes. But Bonnie was in jail in Kaufman all that spring. The legend of this notorious female criminal was growing, with legend outpacing fact.

11

LIFE AND DEATH ON THE ROAD

In the summer of 1932, with Bonnie free and Clyde on the run, life on the road really began. They were joined again by Raymond Hamilton, the young man who'd left after the $33,000 bank robbery. They committed a string of small robberies, none earning very much money. In early August, a train station job brought them $440, a pretty good take.

Bonnie went back to her mother's house, still trying to hide from her that she was back with Clyde. In fact, she told her mother she had a job in Wichita Falls, Texas, when she was really on the road with Clyde.

On August 5, Clyde, Hamilton, and a gang member named Ross Dyer went to Stringtown, Oklahoma. They were not there to rob anyone, just to have some fun. A town dance was being held, complete with band, girls to dance with, and illegal whiskey to drink. (Prohibition, a law that banned the sale of alcohol, was still the law of the land at this point in time.) The three men stood out in this small farming town because of their fancy suits and high-powered car. Soon after arriving, a wary sheriff approached the men as they sat in their car drinking. As was usual, he was going to find out who the strangers were. It was a fatal mistake.

Because they knew they were wanted men, Clyde and Hamilton shot the lawman, who was named Charlie Maxwell. Wounded, he fell from the side of the car. Clyde tried to drive away but hit another car. Others appeared to help, including deputy sheriff Eugene Moore. In another hail of bullets, Clyde and Hamilton killed Moore, the first law officer the Barrow gang had gunned down (Maxwell would later recover from his wounds).

The two men escaped and continued on the run for days, switching cars often and hiding out when they could. Ross Dyer, however, never made it out of Stringtown. He was captured that evening and probably revealed Clyde and Hamilton as his partners in crime. The next morning Clyde called on Cumie for help. She certainly knew of his criminal life, but this murder was a tragic milestone. For the Bucher murder, he had "just" been the driver. For the Stringtown crime, he was the gunman, and the victim was a peace officer to boot. Marie later wrote that her mother took her son's crime "extremely hard," given that Moore left a wife and two children.[35]

Clyde had to get away, far and fast. But first he sent Raymond Hamilton to pick up Bonnie. She once again lied to her mother about a nonexistent job in another town and climbed into life on the road with Clyde.

Their first trip was due west, in part to escape the manhunt that was underway following the murder of Deputy Moore. They went to New Mexico to visit an aunt of Bonnie's who lived there. After a long drive through the desert, they reached Carlsbad, New Mexico, and Aunt Millie Stamps.

Taking the names James White and Jack Smith, Clyde and Hamilton soon returned to their old ways, committing small crimes nearby for traveling money. They also used Millie's backyard for target practice, which raised her suspicions somewhat. Plus, they arrived with her niece in a nice fancy car but didn't seem to have jobs. After a while she decided to ask the sheriff to visit and check her visitors out.

Deputy Joe Johns arrived but was quickly taken captive by the outlaws. Clyde and Hamilton couldn't afford to have the law poking around. Though they were not wanted in New Mexico, any contact with the Texas authorities would see them arrested. Johns didn't know who these people were and had never heard of the infamous Texans "Bonnie and Clyde." But in moments he found himself in the back seat of the car as the trio kidnapped the lawman and headed, oddly, back to Texas. Within days the car, now beat up and battered from so many miles on dirt roads at high speeds, arrived near San Antonio. Before they reached a populated area, though, Clyde let Johns go. It appeared that Clyde didn't want to kill anyone he didn't have to.

Johns soon let local authorities know that he was safe (he

had been reported murdered back in New Mexico). His descriptions of his captors, however, told Texas officials that Bonnie and Clyde were back. Roadblocks were set up around the area. Clyde and Hamilton had added a second car to their roving escape, and they were nearly caught at one bridge roadblock near Wharton, Texas. Nifty driving by the pair helped them escape once again. They added powerful weapons to their arsenal with the first of what would be several robberies of National Guard armories. The National Guard is a military force that can be called up by the governor of a state in case of civil unrest. The Guard armories stored bigger, higher-caliber weapons than those that were used by police. By taking such guns as the Browning Automatic Rifle (BAR), Clyde was giving himself another edge over the outgunned police.

Hamilton decided to return to Michigan in early September. During this period another group of lawmen entered the picture in a big way. All of the crimes Clyde had committed, most with Bonnie in attendance, had come inside one state or another. The only people who could pursue or arrest him were law officers from those states. But when a car that Clyde stole in Illinois was found in Oklahoma, local officials found clear evidence of who had done the deed. That made the crime an interstate one—that is, crossing state borders during the crime of car theft. The United States had recently created a national Division of Investigation (DOI), led by J. Edgar Hoover. It was in part a response to a wave of state-hopping villains who had popped up in the early 1930s, Bonnie and Clyde among them (see below). The DOI was the forerunner of today's FBI.

BONNIE, CLYDE, AND THE FBI

The group that became the FBI was born in 1908 as an unnamed group of investigators reporting to the Attorney General. In 1909 they were named the Bureau of Investigation and focused on bank-related crimes and intelligence, such as the pursuit of spies. World War I gave the agency its first national test, as they were called on to root out German agents. A young lawyer named J. Edgar Hoover was one of the agents sent by Attorney General Mitchell Palmer on what became the "Palmer Raids." By 1924 Hoover was the director and he quickly expanded the agency's work, focusing on crime related to Prohibition, as well as ongoing intelligence work.

The rise of the gangs in Chicago and other major cities also proved a test for the Bureau.

Hoover was a powerful personality, convinced of the rightness of his causes and choices at all times and not willing to listen to any dissent. One of his major structural changes was to vastly increase the use of fingerprints and other forensic tools, creating the first national database for police. He also set up the first FBI lab for using science to help solve crimes, a regular part of every police agency today.

The mid-1930s put the FBI squarely in the public eye. The rise of state-hopping, gun-toting killers such as John Dillinger, Machine Gun Kelly, and of course Bonnie and Clyde led the public to call for more power in facing this threat. Hoover led the charge to get new laws that let his men pursue these outlaws regardless of where they went in the United States. The FBI Most Wanted list became a regular part of news reporting on crime, and Hoover became the most powerful law enforcement leader in the nation.

He led the FBI until his death in 1972.

For the next several months Bonnie and Clyde led a nomadic life. They traveled from city to city, staying at motels or campgrounds or even car camping by a river. Clyde would boost a few dollars from small stores, but he didn't commit any violent crimes. They visited states all around Texas, then ventured farther north, into Minnesota and Michigan and Ohio. Oddly, they would sometimes stay in an area for several days while they waited for a dry cleaner to freshen up their nicer clothes.

They returned to the Dallas area late in the fall of 1932. Of course, Texas authorities were watching the Barrow and Parker families for any sign of the fugitives. To set up a family gathering, Clyde drove by his father's service station and tossed out a Coke bottle. Inside was a message detailing the meeting places.

While in Dallas, they connected with an old family friend of Clyde's, W. D. Jones. He had been a youngster following the exploits of "Bud and Buck" back in the day. Now sixteen, he was ready to commit to a life of crime on the road.

He soon got more than he bargained for. On Christmas Day 1932, Clyde told W. D. to steal a car for a job. Jones picked one out, but he was not as skilled as Clyde in hot-wiring cars.

It was taking too long, so Clyde came over to help. Then the owner of the car, Doyle Johnson, ran out to stop the thieves. He grabbed Jones while Clyde watched and Bonnie looked on from the waiting car. She moved quickly behind the wheel to prepare their escape. According to Jones, Clyde ran over and shot Johnson in the chest. The pair then stole Johnson's car and Bonnie followed in the trio's car.

As Jones later wrote, Clyde then told him, "You can't go home, boy. You got murder on you, just like me."[36]

~ 12 ~

DEATH TO LAWMEN

The trio of Bonnie, Clyde, and Jones stuck together for the next eight event-packed months. They were at a house in West Dallas when they committed their second murder in as many weeks. And it was by accident. Clyde and Jones were making a late-night visit to a former associate of Clyde's. However, the police were already staking out the house waiting for that associate, a man named Odell Chambless. When Clyde approached, a woman inside shouted a warning to him and he opened fire at the awaiting officers. His first shots with the shotgun he carried missed, but he reloaded quickly as the lawmen approached. He fired again, and Fort Worth city deputy Malcolm Davis was hit in the chest and killed instantly. Meanwhile, Jones was still in the car the gang had arrived in and he fired toward the house and the gun battle, but Bonnie told him to cut it out. Who knew what Jones might hit? While Clyde ran away, Bonnie quickly started the car and raced off. They found Clyde nearby, and once again the Barrow gang was on the run after killing a police officer.

Officers later reported Bonnie's role in the events, one of the first times that she was actually written about in the press as an active member of the gang. Up to that point, she had mostly been the lovesick girlfriend pulled along in the wake of the killer.

The string of murders continued to fill newspapers in Texas and soon in neighboring states. The sensational nature of the girl-on-the-run that was Bonnie created more headlines for the gang than other similar criminals. Reporters were also not afraid to add their own touches to make the stories even more outlandish. Bonnie was several times reported to have shot weapons during the crimes. But Jones and other gang members claim that in all their gunfights, she never shot anything. (She was reported firing at police officers in a 1933 shootout, but accounts of that varied quite a bit.) Jones, however, did write that "She never fired a gun, but I'll say that she was a hell of a loader."[37]

The trio moved from town to town, sometimes staying at quiet motor lodges (Jones usually slept on the floor, while Bonnie and Clyde got the bed) or camping out. They made sure to steal larger cars. One reason was that the powerful cars were perfect for outrunning pursuers. Another was that they had good storage areas. Though the trio were outlaws on the run, they carried a lot of bags of clothes, along with a typewriter for Bonnie, and Clyde's guitar. That's not to mention several cases of weapons.

FORD V-8

Clyde loved big, fast cars. However, there were not many of them out there for him to steal. Then in 1932 Ford Motor Company created a car that turned out to be Clyde's favorite. The Ford V-8 had one of the most powerful engines ever put in a passenger car. Most cars of the time had four or six cylinders. The V-8, as its name said, had eight. That provided not only accelerating power—the car got up to speed quickly, a good thing for a getaway car—but it also had a higher top speed than most police vehicles. Again, great news for robbers, who could simply floor it and outrun pursuit. The four-door models were also very roomy inside and had big windows for good visibility in all directions. "Clyde really banked on them Fords. They was the fastest and the best, and he knew how to drive them with one foot in the gas tank all the time," W. D. Jones wrote later.[38] Clyde made stealing V-8s a signature of his crime spree, and one of them would be the last car he ever drove.

They also played around with a small camera that Clyde had gotten. Jones often acted as the photographer as the pair of lovers/criminals posed with guns, cars, and other props. This seemingly innocent hobby would soon completely change their lives.

Sometimes Bonnie dyed her hair to look a bit different. Jones reported that they made sure not to use their real names when eating out or checking in to lodges. Daddy and Honey were accompanied by Boy, though Jones sometimes called Clyde "Bud," the long-ago Dallas nickname.

On rare occasions they would again sneak home for visits to Dallas. Cumie created a code to let relatives know the trio would be nearby. "I'm making red beans," she'd tell them in a note.

Among their adventures was the kidnapping of yet another lawman, this time Deputy Thomas Persell near Springfield, Missouri. The motorcycle cop was surprised to be greeted by a pair of guns when he pulled their car over. In the ensuing kidnapping, Persell was for a time covered with a blanket while Bonnie kept him quiet by brandishing a pistol. Amazingly, at one point, the car's battery died and Jones forced Persell to walk to a nearby town, remove one from another car, and walk back. It was a surprising show of force by a sixteen-year-old, but when you have the gun, people do what you want.

In March the gang grew. Buck Barrow, Clyde's older brother and criminal inspiration, was released from prison. He immediately rejoined Blanche, who had waited patiently for her man. Though they talked at first of going straight, Clyde had other ideas. He wanted Buck to join him in his dream job: breaking into the Eastham prison farm.

To get his brother and his very reluctant wife to join the expedition, Clyde convinced Buck and Blanche to vacation together. They rented cabins near Joplin, Missouri, and set up housekeeping. Clyde showed Blanche how to make "English peas cooked with a lot of cream and pepper."[39] The group later moved into a rented apartment that included a garage for the cars they were using. They even paid a neighborhood night watchman to add their place to his rounds. Not surprisingly, the group enjoyed the irony of the poor guy not knowing that he was guarding wanted criminals.

After so many months on the road, Bonnie loved having a home of her own. She enjoyed decorating and buying linens. Blanche fumed, hating being around the guns and wanting to get Buck home. But she did enjoy playing with Snowball, a little dog she had found. Clyde and W. D. played a lot of poker and drank a lot of beer.

"All in all, it was just the usual family reunion," Nell Barrow later wrote of this pleasant interlude. "With the exception that Clyde was wanted for three or four murders."[40]

Buck had another motivation—he wanted to convince Clyde to give up his life of crime. Clyde believed that if he was caught, he would be killed or executed. The murders he had committed made him determined to never be captured. Texas had the death penalty and was not afraid to use it. However, Buck was unable to change his younger brother's mind.

Neighbors were quietly watching this unusual group. The five were still strangers, and their late-night ways and high-spending habits caught people's attention. The local police thought something might be up too. They didn't know who the gang was—even by then, details of all their crimes had not made them famous all the way up in Missouri—but they thought they might be bootleggers or part of a ring of car thieves.

On April 13, 1933, five local officers made a raid on the apartment building. They were convinced they had found a local bootlegging group. They got a lot more than they bargained for. The two police cars rolled into the apartment driveway as Clyde and Jones were working on one of their cars. As county constable Wes Harryman got out of his car with his gun out, Clyde fired a shotgun at him. Harryman was hit in the chest and head and would soon die from his wounds. Jones was hit too. A moment later Clyde cut down officer Harry McGinnis, probably dead as he hit the ground.

Clyde continued to fire at the remaining officers, while Buck ran from downstairs to help. Jones ran upstairs, bleeding from his wound. The two women gathered him up and ran back down, piling into one of the gang's cars. They didn't have time to pack or grab anything. . . . They had to go, fast. Blanche did, however, try to run after Snowball, to no avail.

Clyde had to smash into one of the police cars to knock it out of their way, and the gang was off. No one was really after them and they were gone before help could arrive. They had to deal with Jones's wound quickly. As the teenager later wrote, "I got shot in the side at Joplin and my belly ached so bad I thought the bullet had stopped there. Clyde wrapped an elm branch with gauze and pushed it through the hole in my side and out my back. The bullet had gone clean through."[41]

(An interesting side note to this event is an example of how "truth" can be somewhat tricky to pin down in retelling the saga of Bonnie and Clyde. While Jones later wrote—and medical exams proved—that he was shot in the side, in Nell Barrow's retelling of what Bonnie allegedly told her, as printed in *Fugitives*, Jones was shot in the head. Historians looking back at various sets of facts sometimes have to wisely choose which to believe and which not to.[42])

The gang rolled on, putting as much distance as they could between themselves and the events in Joplin. Back at the apartment, the gang had left behind two dead policemen, a ruined dwelling, at least one car, a stash of seven weapons, and evidence of the gang's robberies—diamonds and an empty money bag. Police also found a host of personal possessions.

The most important of those proved to be two rolls of undeveloped film.

13

SUDDEN FAME

Law enforcement swooped in to go over the material left behind in the apartment. After the bodies of Harryman and McGinnis were removed, the police catalogued the guns, ammo, clothing, and other gear. They found a camera and with it two rolls of film. The police made prints, and those prints made history. For the first time, the officers had clear pictures of more than just the mug shots of Clyde Barrow. They also had the first images of Bonnie Parker in her role as part of the gang.

The photos quickly found their way into local newspapers such as the *Joplin Globe* and around the country.

A new device that used telephone lines to send images was coming into use by newspapers nationwide. The photos of Bonnie and Clyde proved just how useful such devices could be. It was one thing to read about the exploits of Bonnie and Clyde. In their home area of Texas and the central southwest, millions had already seen the articles in newspapers. Now they and others around the country saw the pair in a new and oddly attractive light.

The images, most taken by W. D. Jones and Blanche Barrow, showed Clyde the killer and his blond "moll" in a variety of casual poses. Other photos showed Jones posing in front of a car festooned with guns. Blanche and Buck posed for a photo in a tight hug. From what the pictures showed, it was clear that Bonne and Clyde enjoyed the photo sessions. In one, Bonnie posed holding a shotgun on Clyde. In another, Clyde posed with his guns and his car. There was even a snapshot of the couple in a passionate kiss. This was clearly becoming more than just a crime story. For people around the country swept up in the

Depression, this was suddenly a soap opera, with good and evil, love and death, excitement and danger.

One particular photo stood out and became the most well-known and eventually the most controversial. In it, Bonnie is alone, standing in front of their car. Her left foot is propped up on the front bumper. She holds a large revolver in her right hand. And in her mouth she jauntily clenches a cigar in her teeth. In those days nice women did not smoke cigars. If they smoked, it was cigarettes. Bonnie's aggressive, gun-toting image became the defining visual of the couple's entire time together. Jones later revealed that he had handed Bonnie the cigar as a prop. She also said that she never smoked cigars, only cigarettes. And though she was holding a gun, it was never clear whether or not Bonnie had ever fired a gun during a crime. Along with appearing in newspapers and magazines, the images appeared with other footage in movie newsreels. These short black-and-white features appeared before the regular movie at theaters around the country. In these days before TV, newsreels were the only way that people could see moving images of worlds outside their own. Shown along with images and film of the other infamous gangsters of this mid-1930s period, Bonnie and Clyde soon earned top billing.

AMERICAN OUTLAWS

The 1920s had seen a rise in serious crime in America, led by headline-ready gangsters. The most well-known was Al Capone, leader of Chicago's murderous underworld. He made millions on illegal alcohol sales and other enterprises. Though police knew he was guilty, he was hard to nail down, and he became a well-known public figure. In 1929 he ordered the infamous Saint Valentine's Day Massacre of seven rivals in a Chicago garage. It was such a horrible crime that local and federal agents stepped up their work. By 1931 they had convicted Capone . . . of not paying his income taxes. He ended up in Alcatraz Prison. He died in 1947.

In the 1930s another type of criminal caught the public's eye. With banks around the country suddenly in the role of villain, daring and gun-toting bank robbers became a kind of folk hero. John Dillinger was one of the first and most famous. Named Public Enemy No. 1 by national officials, Dillinger robbed a series of banks in the Midwest in 1932 and 1933. The hunt for him was in headlines and newsreels daily until he was gunned down by police in Chicago in 1934.

Charles "Pretty Boy" Floyd was another machine-gun-wielding bank robber. He pulled off numerous raids, mostly in Oklahoma and neighboring states. His colorful nickname and his use of the deadly new Thompson submachine gun, dubbed the Tommy Gun, made him famous. He was killed in a shootout in Ohio in 1934.

Lone robber Alvin Karpis had already committed several crimes when he joined members of the Barker family, including their mother, Kate "Ma" Barker, in the early 1930s. Their favored crime was kidnapping, but they also committed robberies and murders. Ranging around the upper Midwest, the Karpis-Barker gang was brought to justice late in the 1930s.

Into this tableau of crime and death and sensationalism, eager reporters added Bonnie and Clyde. They stood out from the rest, however, thanks to the presence of Bonnie, the only cute blond female villain. Her status as the girlfriend of the crook, and as a person who was running away from her husband, too, added to their growing legend, which was cemented for all time by the Joplin photos.

The image of a woman gangster as portrayed by Bonnie really turned the duo into national celebrities. Compared to other criminals, they were still not big time. They were deadly, certainly, with at least four killings at their hands in the previous year. But they had not been as successful as people like John Dillinger or Baby Face Nelson. Those gangsters and others focused on banks that held large sums. The scraps that the Barrow gang were pulling in from markets and gas stations were nothing compared to the tens of thousands of dollars collected at gunpoint by others. At one point, Dillinger said that the young criminal pair was "a couple of kids running around stealing grocery money."[43]

But those others were all men (with the exception of Ma Barker). They did not have blond Bonnie at their side. Her presence set the gang above and apart and led directly to their status as folk heroes. The fact that Bonnie and Clyde were unmarried (and in fact, Bonnie was still married to Roy) was particularly shocking. In those days single people did not live together or spend that much time together. Yet here were two attractive people breaking every one of society's rules, from robbery to forbidden love.

People were not directly rooting for the pair, certainly not as they committed murder. But the idea of a man and woman in love, on the run from the cops, living by their wits and guts . . . that had a storybook appeal. Newspapers sensationalized every new story about the gang, hauling out the images from Joplin over and over. If a picture is worth a thousand words, as the old saying goes, then Jones's snapshots wrote a whole book.

While the photos spread rapidly across the land, the Barrow gang raced away to hide, and in the case of Jones, to lick their wounds. It had been a very close call. Clyde's decision to open fire immediately upon seeing the police in Joplin would become his calling card. It was also a clear signal that what he had said after he got out of Eastham was true: He was never going back and would die rather than face prison again.

14

THE ACCIDENT

Two weeks later the Barrow group had made it to Louisiana. In the small town of Renton they stole a car as a prelude to a bank job. Things quickly got out of hand. Jones was spotted stealing the car by its owner, H. D. Darby. A woman named Sophia Stone offered to chase the stolen car with Darby. Jones got away from them, but amazingly, Clyde and Buck pulled the couple over to find out what was happening. When told they were chasing their stolen car, Clyde knew what was up and kidnapped the pair. For miles, the car, packed with six people now, rolled through the Louisiana back roads. Clyde ranted at Jones for messing up and threatened the kidnap victims. Bonnie, for her part, apparently chatted away like it was a drive in the country. Eventually, they left the couple by the side of the road; Clyde even gave Darby five dollars to help him get a ride back to Renton. Their story quickly was sent around the country. (The media-hungry Ms. Stone was particularly cooperative with reporters, adding new bits to her story with each retelling.) With the idea of two people escaping death at the hands of the notorious bandits, and with photos of that same pair to go along with it, it was yet another chapter in the growing saga.

On the run, they drove and drove. Blanche later wrote that they rambled through nine states during their flight.

Bonnie and Clyde didn't find Jones again for several weeks. He apparently went back to Texas. The remaining four spent May in the north, visiting Indiana and Minnesota. They were foiled in one bank robbery attempt and successful in a minor one. In late May they returned to Texas and set up a secret meeting with their families near Dallas. The Coke bottle was thrown, the message went out, and the Barrows and Parkers had a reunion that any lawman would have loved to crash. Cumie and Marie talked about the party in *Fugitives*, while Blanche gave her version in her memoirs. The stories were of a typical family gathering, for the most part. There was lemonade and beer, beans and corn bread. The younger kids raced about, and the older women teased Blanche about what she was wearing. Bonnie and Clyde had brought presents for the family, passing out money, including a special gift for one niece's birthday. What made it different from most family gatherings was that the money came from robberies and the stories told as the sun set in the west were about kidnappings and shootouts.

Soon after the gathering Bonnie and Clyde reunited with Jones and headed back out on the road. Blanche and Buck, to Cumie's sadness, joined them.

On June 10, 1933, for the first time Clyde's great driving skills failed him. Buck and Blanche had gone ahead in another car. As Clyde drove Bonnie and Jones through rural Wellington, Texas, he did not see signs indicating road construction ahead. At full speed, the car soared off a short drop. It landed with a terrible crash and soon caught fire. Though Clyde was ejected from the car as it rolled, he was not seriously hurt. Jones was in the back seat, dazed but uninjured. Bonnie, however, was in trouble (although, again, another account says that Clyde was still in the car after the crash). In the front passenger seat she was being burned by acid from the car battery that had broken in the crash. Her screams and the noise of the crash brought help from a nearby house. The people there carried Bonnie to safety. One of the women put baking soda on the burns, which probably saved Bonnie's leg. Still, the burns were terrible, "down to the bone," Jones later recalled.[44] It was a terrible injury, one that should have been dealt with in a hospital. But Bonnie and Clyde could not just show up hoping for help. In fact, after Clyde went back to the car to see if he could get their guns, one of the men in the house became suspicious and drove away to get help. The rescuers soon found themselves under threat, as Clyde knew that once the law arrived, there would be trouble.

When two police officers arrived, Clyde and Jones took their weapons at gunpoint. Then they handcuffed the men and bundled them into a car from the farmhouse. As Bonnie, in great pain, lay atop the kidnapped cops, Clyde drove them all to safety, reconnecting with Buck and Blanche in Oklahoma. They released the police unharmed and fled. The group finally found a small lodge in Arkansas where they were able to get rooms without being identified. Clyde even managed to get medical help for Bonnie, finally, telling a local doctor that "his wife" had been injured in a camp stove explosion. As Bonnie's wounds healed slowly, with help from fresh bandages put on by the doctor's unsuspecting daughter, the group was in danger all the time. But Bonnie just could not have made it stuck in a car for hours on end. In fact, for the rest of her short life, Bonnie was severely hobbled. She had trouble walking and was often in pain. "When she was so bad at first, we had to carry her to the toilet and take her off when she finished and put her back in bed," Jones later wrote.[45]

They remained hidden in the lodge for weeks. At one point Clyde even snuck back to Dallas and got Bonnie's sister, Billie Jean, to come and help him care for Bonnie. (Nell reported her brother "sobbed like a little boy" while bemoaning Bonnie's condition.[46]) Buck and Jones made attempts to get the money the group still needed by pulling off small robberies nearby. One such attempt did not go so well. At one point they managed to steal all of twenty dollars from a store in Fayetteville, Arkansas. During the chase and gunfight that followed, Buck shot Marshall Henry Humphrey, who died two weeks later of his injuries. It was time to get on the move again, so the Barrow gang, with Billie Jean sent home, went back on the road.

The combination of the death of yet another lawman and the new notoriety brought by the photos made police that much more determined to capture the Barrow gang. The net began tightening, even as the Barrow cars raced through the southern night.

~ 15 ~

AMBUSHES

The chase for the Barrow gang intensified. Police all around Missouri now had photos and detailed descriptions wired out from Joplin. Up to this point police had been hampered because they did not all know what the outlaws looked like other than years-old mug shots. Also, police in those days rarely shared information. The days of instant communication and sharing of information were in the future.

The outrages of the Barrow gang called for new tactics,

however, and a statewide hunt was well underway when Clyde arrived at a motor lodge in Platte City, Missouri, about 175 miles north of Joplin. Clyde might have thought he had put enough distance between them and the Joplin shootout, but he was wrong.

The owners of the Red Crown motor lodge welcomed the couples, who signed in as married under false names. Jones was supposedly Buck's brother. To the gang's surprise, lodge owner N. D. Houser wrote down the license plate (which was stolen) of their car (which was also stolen). Given recent and well-publicized events, the lodge owners were a bit concerned. The bad news for Clyde and his cronies was that the Red Crown was, as author Jeff Guinn wrote, "a gathering place for local cops and the state highway patrol."[47] Houser told visiting officers about his new guests and the suspicions grew. Things heated up when the license plate number came back as belonging to a stolen car from Enid, Oklahoma. Missouri officials knew who they had—the Barrow gang.

With a seeming opportunity to capture the notorious outlaws, local law enforcement got ready. The sheriff had read about the gang's firepower, so he requested heavy-duty armored cars and high-powered weapons from the county. He got the former and not the latter. The milling crowd of officers at the small motor lodge finally caught Blanche's attention (she was the one sent out by Clyde and Buck for food), but the men didn't think much of her report.

Law enforcement figured that the gang was becoming suspicious, however, and thirteen officers gathered early in the morning of July 20. Unlike previous attempts to capture Clyde and his gang, police were armed and ready. Some had machine guns, others powerful shotguns. A few hid behind heavy metal shields. The armored car was rolled into position to block the garage attached to one cabin, where the gang's car was parked. As soon as the officers knocked on the cabin where Blanche and Buck were living, Clyde, W. D., and Buck started shooting. Once again, Clyde would go down fighting; giving up was never an option for him.

Jones was sent to start the car, sheltered in the garage. But even there bullets from the police were pinging in all directions. To clear the way, Clyde blasted repeated shots through the garage door. The BAR he fired was so powerful that rounds went through the metal sheeting of the armored car and hit the deputy driving it. Wounded, the officer pulled the car away from the door. That gave Jones and Bonnie a chance to get into the car and start it up. The problem for the gang was that Blanche and Buck were across a wide walkway in the other cabin. They would have to run through a hail of gunfire to reach the car and possible escape. As Clyde and W. D. fired at the officers, Blanche and Buck sprinted out.

Buck was struck in the head by a bullet. He fell immediately to the ground. He was dazed but conscious; the bullet had gone across and through his forehead. Amazingly Blanche was not hit and was able to pull the heavier Buck across the rest of the walkway and into the car. As Clyde gunned the V-8 Ford out of the garage, dozens more bullets peppered the car. One smashed the back window. Glass shards flew through the air and speared Blanche in both eyes. Clyde didn't look back. He floored it.

The next hours were desperate and hair-raising. Clyde searched on a variety of back roads for a clean getaway route. Buck bled copiously in the back seat. Shockingly, the bullet had gone into his skull at one point near his temple and gone out another in his forehead. Both holes remained and were bleeding.

For her part, Blanche could see some shadows and light but was otherwise blinded, at least temporarily. Bonnie tried to help Blanche while also helping Clyde navigate. They had no food, no water, and little money. They did slip into a drugstore for some bandages. Guinn reported that the trail of bloody bandages used and discarded for Buck's horrible wound turned into an easy trail for pursuers to follow.[48] Bonnie's burned leg called for more bandages, along with ointment. Late on the night of July 20, the group finally found a place to rest, a place called Dexfield Park in Iowa. They had driven nearly two hundred rough and painful miles. The law was not far behind.

Buck was in bad shape. They made a sort of bed for him with car seats and cushions. They even dug a grave for him in case the worst happened. As Clyde helped Buck, Blanche reported in her memoirs that she tried to convince W. D. to leave the gang while he could. Clyde chimed in that W. D. was heading for the electric chair thanks to his involvement in several killings. Still just seventeen, Jones was looking for a way out.

Over the next several days the group camped out in the woods of the parkland. They made quick trips into nearby towns for food and bandages, making sure to cover up or not wear any bloodstained clothing. Clyde even got a block of ice to help with Buck's swelling head. Eventually, however, they were noticed in the park and a local deputy reported what he saw through binoculars to the county sheriff. Within hours, representatives of a half-dozen police agencies were heading to the park. They were not alone, as more than two dozen armed local people joined the unofficial posse. This was not 2017—police in this case welcomed the help of more guns on their side, especially given the Barrow gang's history of firepower and fearless killing.

On July 24, within minutes of the arrival of the large group near the gang's campsite, a massive gunfight broke out. Hundreds of bullets and shotgun pellets flew through the air. Buck, of course, could do little to help. Clyde and W. D. blasted away but both were hit, Clyde in the left arm and W. D. in the chest. Even Bonnie caught some shotgun pellets in her side.

As the gunfire popped around them, Clyde told everyone to get in the car. He fired it up, but it quickly stalled in the mud and brush of the park. They clambered out again, Blanche pulling Buck along with her. Clyde, Bonnie, and Jones dove for the cover of some trees. Clyde would have to leave his older brother behind.

Blanche stayed with Buck, who somehow managed to fire off some shots from his position near a tree. The posse returned fire and Buck was hit by several bullets, but even those did not kill him. Moments later, Blanche and Buck surrendered. The local news photographers captured the grim scene as the grievously wounded Buck was taken in. Blanche frantically tried to get at him as she, too, was put in handcuffs.

In the woods Clyde and Jones were helping the still-crippled Bonnie through the brush. They reached a shallow river and forded across. "I was carrying [Bonnie] on my back, half-stumbling, half-swimming," remembered Jones.[49] The trio reached a farm owned by the Feller family and forced them at gunpoint to help. Only Clyde and Jones knew that the pistol Clyde brandished was empty. The Fellers were forced to put fuel into one of their cars and then help the injured Bonnie get in. Then the family watched the most famous outlaws in Missouri drive away from their farm. The ensuing hunt now included airplanes, dogs, cars, and multiple police agencies. However, Bonnie and Clyde got away again.

Buck Barrow was not so lucky.

Back in Dallas, Cumie Barrow packed to head north to see her son. "I don't care what people say, they're my boys and I love them," she told a Dallas newspaper.[50] She made it to Iowa in time to be with Buck when he died of his wounds on July 29. Blanche was not with her husband; she was in jail. Repeated interrogations by officials had yielded little information. A patch covered her more seriously injured left eye (she never did regain sight in that eye). Even J. Edgar Hoover of the young FBI came to question her. Within weeks, she was on trial for her part in the Red Crown shootout and was later sentenced to ten years in prison. The Barrow gang was shrinking fast.

16

ON THE RUN AGAIN

Following the death of Buck and imprisonment of Blanche, the gang was down to three in the latter part of 1933. For most of August, Bonnie, Clyde, and Jones drove and drove. Wounded and hunted, they traveled as far north as Minnesota and as far south as Mississippi following the Iowa ambush. In Illinois, Clyde and Jones broke into a National Guard Armory to obtain more BARs and ammunition. They made a series of smaller robberies to pick up traveling money. Their long trail eventually brought them back home yet again. Cumie and her family welcomed Bonnie and Clyde back with open arms.

Jones was not part of this happy reunion. He had left his companions in September, returning to Houston. "I'd had enough blood and hell," he later said of his decision.[51] However, he was later arrested in November for his part in the killing of Malcolm Davis in Texas, which was actually committed by Clyde. He gave a statement to police that was a mix of fact and fiction. For example, Jones said he was chained up in motels so he could not get away or was forced at gunpoint to take part in crimes. He also said he was "unconscious" during parts of shootouts. In other places, he admitted to taking part in robberies and particularly in the death of Doyle Johnson, his first deadly criminal act. He also provided to a curious public more details of life on the run with the most famous criminal couple in the country. Clyde later told family members that he had no problem with Jones trying to lessen his role in the gang's activities, saying "the kid had done the smart thing."[52]

(Jones's statement to Dallas police was later typed up. Several pages from the statement can be seen at the Portal to Texas

History website and are great artifacts of the times. The entire document was made public and added eyewitness fuel to the ever-growing romantic story of the doomed lovers/outlaws.[53])

Surprisingly, the police in Dallas were no longer keeping watch on the Barrow and Parker families. Still, Bonnie and Clyde lived mostly in their car or camped out, fearing that if they stayed in their homes they would be caught and their families put in danger. This time around, instead of receiving gifts of money and presents as in years past, the families had to supply their fugitive children with food and medicine. They even got a pair of crutches for Bonnie to use.

Family stories of these meetings often remarked on how awful Bonnie looked. Her leg continued to ail her and she usually had to keep it tucked under her. She still had great difficulty walking. The pain led her to drink too much as well, and the cute little blonde of earlier years was disappearing.

The author Jeff Guinn also writes of a "pervading sense of doom" to these family gatherings.[54] With the death of Buck, the reality of the probable end of their lives hit the couple hard. Their family shared that doomed feeling. Clyde was clearly not going to survive for very long with so many people after him and with his stated choice to go down fighting. He still tried to get Bonnie to leave him. At one point he said he would write a letter absolving her of any blame if she'd get more medical help and give up. But she refused and stuck by her man. Instead, Clyde told his mother what he wanted on his grave's headstone: "Gone but Not Forgotten." Still, Clyde continued to commit crimes to pull in needed money, recruiting new accomplices from Dallas.

Bonnie got more bad news in October with the death of a young niece and then a nephew from childhood illnesses. She had longed for children in her younger days, and these deaths on top of Buck and everything else made her very depressed. More and more, the family tried to get the despondent Bonnie to give up on Clyde. She once again stuck it out, even asking to be buried together, so sure was she of her coming death.

On November 22, the family gathered once again to celebrate Cumie's birthday. Their long respite from being bothered by police ended.

No one is quite sure how they were tipped off, but police heard about the birthday gathering and were ready. Four officers were lying in wait for the pair to arrive for their meeting with Cumie. As soon as the officers saw Clyde start the car, they let loose with pistols, a rifle, and a machine gun. They fired dozens of bullets, many of which hit the car, but yet another fusillade ended without the capture of the pair. Clyde's driving skill once again guided them out of danger, though both were slightly wounded by bullets and flying glass as they raced away. Subsequently, family members said that Clyde returned later to the area and waited for his own chance to ambush the sheriff, Smoot Schmid. Shooting at Clyde was one thing. But at this latest ambush, his mother and sisters had been nearby. Clyde was angry, but he never followed through on his threat.

(Even this close call with death at the hands of police could not keep Clyde from seeing his mother. From the date of the shooting through the following March, Clyde returned again and again to see her. Guinn reports that Cumie "recorded the dates of Clyde's visits, marking them on a wall in the Barrow family shack on Eagle Ford Road." The list included nearly twenty such visits, each of which put Clyde at risk of capture.[55])

He did follow through with one threat he had made nearly

three years earlier. When he heard that Raymond Hamilton, a former associate, was in prison at the Eastham farm where Clyde had spent time, Clyde recalled a desperate plan. With the help of new gang members, he would break Hamilton out of Eastham.

17

THE EASTHAM RAID

When he was being brutally beaten at the Eastham prison back in Texas, Clyde had planned to come back one day and exact revenge. He finally got his chance in early 1934, nearly three years after he had left there with a mutilated foot and a damaged soul.

Hamilton's brother Floyd and a recently released prisoner named James Mullen contacted Clyde. Hamilton had been bragging for weeks that his old buddy Clyde would break him out.

"I'll be out of here in a few weeks," he said. "There ain't no prison that can hold me, not while I got Clyde Barrow to help me out on the lam."[56]

In early January they sent word that they were ready to go, with Clyde's help. Ray Hamilton had a plan to stash some guns for an Eastham work crew to find. The inmates would use the guns to free themselves, and then Clyde would be there to act as the getaway driver. Though Clyde did not like this particular plan, he finally agreed to it. On January 15, he was in place when Raymond Hamilton and inmate Joe Palmer got the guns and shot two guards. They raced for the car, along with three other inmates, one of whom was Henry Methvin, who would later play a deadly role in the Bonnie and Clyde story.

Clyde fired his BAR back over the fleeing prisoners' heads toward the guards while Bonnie, along for the ride as always, honked the horn as a signal. One of the prisoners just kept running, but the rest packed into the Ford Clyde had brought. He had not expected so many escapees, so it was a tight fit—two even went into the trunk.[57] They quickly pulled away from the guards, who were only on horseback.

During their flight, they stopped for gas. Having heard the news on his radio, the attendant filling the tank asked, "Did you hear about Raymond Hamilton escaping from prison?" He also said that Bonnie and Clyde had done the deed. Clyde probably enjoyed answering with surprise, "No, really?"[58]

The group was soon safely away from the area of the prison. The next day they got new clothes and ditched their prison overalls. Hamilton took up his familiar place at Clyde's side as a trusted lieutenant. Methvin saw the wisdom of teaming up and joined the gang. Hilton Bybee was another escapee—he had been swapped in for Raymond Fults at the last moment—and he chose to stick around too. Palmer, an experienced criminal though in poor health, made a fourth. The Barrow gang was restocked and ready for action.

More men meant more guns meant bigger targets. In the coming weeks they robbed a bank in Iowa and another in Oklahoma. They also hit an armory to stock up on weapons. At a third bank robbery in Texas, Clyde reportedly gave back money he had taken from a customer after the man claimed he had earned it digging ditches. "We don't want your money," Clyde allegedly said. "Just the bank's."[59] The bank jobs were some of the most lucrative in Clyde's checkered criminal history. However, the gang's time together was short-lived. By early March, arguing over money—and over the role of Raymond's girlfriend, a wannabe Bonnie named Mary O'Dare—had increased. Hamilton left with Mary. Bybee had split off earlier.

Not long after he left, a letter Hamilton wrote to his lawyer that criticized Clyde was printed in Texas newspapers. Clyde read it and became so angry he wrote a letter of his own, firing back at Hamilton. In part it read, "It makes me sick to see a yellow punk like that playing baby and making a jury cry over him. If he was half as smart as me the officers couldn't catch him either."[60]

In late March, Clyde allegedly took part in one of the more brazen killings in his short career. During his time at Eastham, Palmer had been routinely terrorized by another inmate, Wade McNabb. This reminded Clyde, of course, of Ed Crowder, who had done the same to him. Together, Palmer and Clyde plotted to kill McNabb soon after he was released from Eastham on a sixty-day pass. (According to a story later told by Ray Fults, Palmer actually paid for an attorney to get McNabb released.[61]) The pair tracked him to the Houston area and apparently kidnapped him from a dominoes parlor. McNabb's body was found on April 3, 1934, after police followed clues in an anonymous note. The skull was smashed and the body had several bullet wounds. Though it was never proven, this was almost certainly the work of Clyde and Palmer. It stands out because, other than Crowder, all of Clyde's killings came during or around his crime spree and not in such a cold-blooded manner.

Soon after the Eastham raid, Clyde's fame came back to haunt him. Though he had not come up with the plan, he (and "cigar-smoking, gun-toting" Bonnie[62]) were given all the credit for the prison break in the media and by prison officials. The head of the Texas prisons was Lee Simmons, and he took the attack on the prison—and the death of one of the guards the inmates had shot—personally. Simmons looked at all the work that had been done, most of it poorly, to track down Clyde and his gang. He saw that one of the biggest reasons for their long record of escapes was the lack of a central focus on tracking them. With the help of the governor of Texas, he hired Frank Hamer, who was named "Special Escape Investigator for the Texas Prison System."[63]

18

HERE COMES HAMER

Frank Hamer seems, looking back, like the kind of person a novelist would make up. But he was as real as Bonnie and Clyde. Hamer had been a Texas Ranger for decades, part of an elite force that acted as state police in what was then the largest US state. The Rangers were so tough that one of their famous slogans was "One riot, one Ranger." He wore the Texas star for twenty-eight years and in that time allegedly killed as many as forty men that he was seeking. There is no way to pin down the exact number, but a reporter who spoke with Hamer's son once got an estimate of "less than a dozen."[64]

At six foot three and more than two hundred pounds, Hamer was a big, tough Texan. He grew up in the rough farm-and-cattle country of West Texas, learning to live off the land while he did his work. He got his start in law enforcement with the Rangers in 1906, patrolling vast areas on horseback. Over the next two decades he was in and out of the Ranger corps, leaving it to take temporary jobs with local police. Among his most famous escapades was defending an African-American prison inmate from a lynch mob in 1930.

In a job that called for toughness, wits, and a willingness to shoot, Hamer was almost unequaled.

(In the 1967 movie about Bonnie and Clyde [for more, see page 137], Hamer was portrayed almost as a villain. By giving him the "bad guy" role in a movie about outlaw killers, his reputation suffered during the 1960s and 1970s. The 2016 book *Texas Ranger: The Epic Life of the Man Who Killed Bonnie & Clyde*, by John Boessenecker, presented a broader picture of Hamer's long career and tried to put his actions in 1934 in more context.)

Simmons gave Hamer his marching orders. He wanted the lawman to put Bonnie and Clyde "on the spot and shoot everyone in sight."[65] It was certainly a sign of the times that before and after the death of Bonnie and Clyde, there was very little, if any, public outcry at police methods. Imagine the discussion today if a police squad were assigned to "shoot everyone."

To fulfill his mission, Hamer brought in Dallas deputy Bob Alcorn, who knew Clyde and had tracked him often in recent years. They were later joined by Ted Hinton, a Dallas deputy who had actually shot at Clyde during the Dallas-area roadside ambush around Cumie's birthday. Another ex-Ranger, Manny Gault, became the fourth member of Hamer's central crew.

Starting in March 1934, Hamer studied all that he could about the Barrow gang's activities and methods. He saw that they often sprinted north after crimes in and around Texas, so he concentrated most of his attention on those areas.

Hamer also knew that figuring out where Bonnie and Clyde would be at a specific time was the key to capturing them—or having a chance to kill them. To do that, he believed he needed an inside man. One of his first trips was to Louisiana, where he met with the Methvin family. He offered a full pardon for Henry to Henry's parents in exchange for help setting up the wanted pair. At the time, it was a good plan, though there is dispute as to whether Henry even knew about it. Methvin's family wanted their son free of trouble and they soon agreed to help Hamer set up the outlaw couple.

⤙ 19 ⤚

HIGHWAY DEATH

While Hamer was gathering his forces, Clyde finally went too far, at least as far as the general public was concerned. He was certainly not beloved by this point, having killed several policemen. But he remained a figure of great popular interest, as much for his ongoing love of Bonnie as for his criminal deeds. The duo's exploits continued to gain headlines, newsreel coverage, and breathless radio reporting. But on Easter Sunday 1934, Clyde, along with Henry Methvin, committed two of the worst killings in the Barrow gang's deadly life.

Bonnie, Clyde, Palmer, and Methvin rolled through Dallas that holiday morning, with the loving couple aiming for another family visit. They set up in a small park near a highway northwest of Dallas close to a town called Grapevine. Palmer was sent back into Dallas to tell the families where Bonnie and Clyde were waiting. He hitchhiked there and wound up missing the action that followed.

The day was warm, but not too hot yet for a Texas spring. Clyde was so relaxed that he snoozed in the car's back seat. Methvin stood a kind of watch, his BAR ready. Bonnie played in the grass with Sonny Boy, a pet rabbit she was planning to give to her mother in honor of the holiday.

Driving past on the other side of the highway, a pair of Texas Highway Patrol motorcycle officers saw the dark Ford V-8, sporting bright yellow wheel rims, parked in the brush. They decided to turn around and investigate. They were not on the specific lookout for Bonnie and Clyde, but the whole Dallas area was constantly aware of the presence of the pair, along with Ralph Hamilton and other villains.

E. Wheeler was the senior member of the pair of officers. His partner, H. D. Murphy, was actually on his very first patrol. It would be his last. Methvin spotted the pair heading toward the car and woke Clyde, who quickly snatched up his shotgun and whispered, "Let's take them."[66] Methvin interpreted that as "kill," when in fact Clyde probably meant "kidnap," as he had with several other law officers in recent months. The misinterpretation turned into chaos.

Methvin leveled the BAR and shot Wheeler in the chest, instantly killing the patrolman, who was engaged to be married. Clyde was probably very angry with his partner, but the die was cast and he raised his shotgun at Murphy. The young officer didn't even have his own shotgun loaded, and as he grabbed for the shells in his pocket, Clyde blasted him. Methvin then approached the dying officer and fired at least two more shots into him.

In seconds the trio was back in the V-8 heading north toward Oklahoma. They still believed that changing states after a crime would make pursuit difficult.

In the aftermath back at the side of the highway, several strands of the Bonnie and Clyde story came together. First, a couple who had heard the shots as they drove by had returned to see Methvin fire the coup de grâce bullets at Murphy. The couple, a Mr. and Mrs. Fred Giggal, immediately drove away. They reported that "the taller of the two men" had fired the additional shots.[67] However, another witness told a different story, one that matched popular misperception. William Schieffer owned a farm that was more than two hundred yards away from the shooting site. He claimed that he had seen a man and a woman do the shooting and that the woman had fired the extra shots. Schieffer's graphic description of Murphy's head bouncing "off the ground like a rubber ball"[68] was just the kind of detail reporters loved, even if it was not true.

As the police gathered evidence, they found lemon peels in the grass. One patrolman knew that Bonnie had a habit of chewing the fruit bits to mask the smell of whiskey on her breath. A bottle was found with a fingerprint of Methvin's. No matter whether Schieffer's specific story was true or not, the facts now all added up to what authorities feared: Two more had died at the hands of Bonnie and Clyde.

In fact, the false reports from Schieffer became the first time that Bonnie was publicly reported as having actually killed anyone.

As author Jeff Guinn points out, "Overnight, [Bonnie] was newly perceived as a kill-crazy floozy."[69] Murphy's grief-stricken fiancée added a note of real emotion to the fading fantasy of Bonnie as a loving girl following her man. (The fiancée, Marie Tullis, was seen in her wedding gown at the officer's funeral several days later; their wedding date had been April 13.) The press attention to the twin killings rose to a fever pitch. Newsreels captured the highway scene of the dead officers, while the Joplin photos once again sped around the country.

Police, meanwhile, now had even more intense reasons for hunting down the pair. They had killed two more of their own. Rewards were offered by the highway patrol and the governor's office. Frank Hamer and his crew were on the trail already, finding places that Bonnie and Clyde (along with Methvin and the probably frightened Sonny Boy) had stopped in Oklahoma. Amazingly, in Durant, Oklahoma, one of the two Hamer cars saw the couple driving past in the opposite direction. By the time they had turned around and found their partners, the lawmen couldn't find the outlaws again.

Two days later, April 6, a different pair of officers did find the fleeing felons. Outside of Commerce, Texas, Clyde had to stop the car to wait out yet another rainstorm. As he rolled to the side of the road, the car ended up in a low ditch. The heavy rain had fallen for the past couple of days and the all-dirt roads were now mostly mud. Even the powerful Ford could not power through the muck. On that morning they were waiting for the rain to let up so they could get unstuck when local police chief Percy Boyd and deputy Cal Campbell approached their car. Campbell recognized that one of the men in the car had a gun and pulled his pistol. It was too late. Clyde and Methvin opened up with the BARs. Campbell was killed by the first shots. Boyd was grazed in the head and fell. Clyde ordered Henry to drag the bleeding Boyd into the car. Clyde then used the rifle to force onlookers to push and drag his car from the mud. According to the witnesses, he called out, "Boys, one good man has already been killed, and if you don't follow orders, others are liable to be."[70] It took the arrival of a passing truck before the car could be pulled free using chains.

For hours the car then cruised north, trying to reach Oklahoma and then Kansas. Bonnie chatted with Boyd and even made him a bandage for his wound. Clyde refused to take the pocket cash from Boyd when they needed gas money, instead breaking open a gum machine, while also providing the lawman with a clean shirt to replace his bloodied one.

Eventually, they let Boyd go. As he was being let out, he asked Bonnie, who at least had treated him well, if she wanted to tell people anything.

She famously told him one thing: "Tell them I don't smoke cigars."[71]

Bonnie told her mother during a future meeting that her antismoking note was "in all the Oklahoma newspapers!"[72] But that little tidbit did not dim the tide of horror that followed the highway murders. The triple killings were the last straw as far as the public and the police were concerned. Following this incident, Bonnie and Clyde were no longer being chased to be captured. They were being chased to be killed. And in Frank Hamer, authorities finally had a man who was ready, willing, and able to do just that. What Clyde did not know and probably never found out was that he was riding around Texas with the man who would sell him down the river.

20

THE NET CLOSES

Even as Hamer marshaled his forces, Bonnie and Clyde could not resist the pull of family. In April they met several times with the Barrow clan. Bonnie finally was able to pass along Sonny Boy to her family. It was another strange family circumstance, as Clyde wanted to make sure everyone knew Bonnie had not shot anyone but that he had killed Officer Murphy. He complained to his family about Methvin's trigger-happy ways. During one visit he was happy to learn that his old partner Raymond Hamilton was once again in jail, having been caught after a bank robbery. Clyde even wrote a long and snarky letter to Hamilton, accusing of him of various misdeeds against himself and the gang and saying that "you can never expect the least of sympathy or assistance from me."[73]

The connections to family remained deep throughout their criminal lives. As his sister Nell later wrote in *Fugitives*, "I know this all sounds incongruous, but remember that even the worst criminals have families that they love." She did add that they didn't like what Bonnie and Clyde were doing ("the entire business nearly drove us crazy").[74]

In late April they robbed a bank in Iowa and then stole yet another Ford V-8 in Topeka, Kansas. That particular car would soon become nationally famous.

A few days after that theft, Palmer decided to head north. He wanted to see the Chicago World's Fair. Bonnie and Clyde were heading south to visit with Methvin's family. On previous trips there, they had enjoyed the area. During a visit with their families in April, Clyde had actually talked about buying land in Louisiana.

That's where they were headed in mid-May, to see the

Methvins. The couple even took up brief residence in a small cottage and spent time with Methvin's extended family, who apparently didn't mind having the well-known outlaws around. Henry, of course, was not exactly a choirboy.

Hamer had been waiting for this moment to arrive. He had expected the couple to head to Louisiana. Lee Simmons later said that Hamer had been sure to show his forces active in Texas and Oklahoma to get Clyde to think he could ditch the Hamer posse by going south.

The agreement to pardon Methvin in Texas was still in place with his parents and with Texas and Louisiana government officials. The local sheriff was in on Hamer's plan and didn't bother the outlaws-in-hiding. On May 21, Methvin's parents got Henry alone to confirm that things were all set. All he had to do was get away from the couple, who had agreed to catch up with him later at the Methvin family house. Later that day, when the trio went to the larger city of Shreveport, Henry ditched Bonnie and Clyde. Now alone, they knew to head back to Henry's parents' house.

Hamer was not far behind Methvin, and once he saw that the

Louisiana man had finally left the outlaw couple on their own, he knew it was time to go in for the kill. But the couple didn't come back that day, May 22, and in fact Henry ended up meeting with them in the evening. The fatal showdown was pushed back a day.

Hamer called his son Frank Jr. the night before and said, "The chickens are coming home to roost tomorrow about nine o'clock."[75]

BONNIE'S FINAL POEM

In early May, Bonnie and Clyde had visited Dallas again, still talking up the Louisiana relocation. Bonnie gave her mother a copy of what would become her most famous poem (see Appendix for full text). It proved to contain deadly foreshadowing. It ends with these lines:

> *They don't think they're too tough or desperate,*
>
> *They know that the law always wins;*
>
> *They've been shot at before,*
>
> *But they do not ignore*
>
> *That death is the wages of sin.*

Some day they'll go down together;

And they'll bury them side by side;

To few it'll be grief

To the law a relief

But it's death for Bonnie and Clyde.

21

A VIOLENT END

Thanks to Ivy Methvin (Henry's dad), the Hamer posse and the local lawmen who'd been added to the shooting party knew that Bonnie and Clyde would be driving down the road to the Methvin farm on the morning of Wednesday, May 23, 1934. Hamer pulled a fast one on Methvin, though, asking him at the last minute to be present at the site chosen for the ambush. It was a straight part of the road, and Hamer worried that lead-foot Clyde would be moving too fast. They decided to park Methvin's truck by the side of the road and hope Clyde would slow or stop when he saw the vehicle. Methvin was worried that if it didn't work, Clyde would take revenge on him and his family. In the end it was just Methvin's truck that was needed, though he was nearby.

Knowing Clyde's ability to slip out of ambushes, the men, now six in all, came prepared with an arsenal of high-powered weapons. There were rifles and a machine gun and a powerful shotgun. Two had the BAR rifles that Clyde himself preferred. Hinton was also lugging a small movie camera that he had been carrying since he started working with Hamer. They wanted a record of what they hoped to do.

They set up alongside the road and near where Methvin's truck was stopped, arriving very early in the morning so they would be ready when the couple's Ford barreled through. The truck was made to look like it had trouble. It was put up on a jack and a tire was removed.

Setting up a screen of branches and bushes, the lawmen hunkered down to wait. Hamer took the position of "last man," farthest up the road. Armed with two powerful guns, he would make sure Clyde didn't escape, no matter what.

Several other cars passed as the men waited, but Ivy went out to make sure folks just kept moving, telling the drivers he didn't need help.

Just past nine fifteen, the men farthest down the road heard the sound of the V-8 engine, and they all knew it was time.

The plan was that Hamer would challenge Clyde when he stopped at the "broken-down" truck. But local deputy Prentiss Oakley could not wait. As soon as the car rolled to a stop near the truck, he fired several rounds with his rifle, striking the car in multiple places. One round pierced the glass and then Clyde's head.

Clyde Barrow was dead.

Now that the car had no living driver, it rolled slowly forward as Clyde's foot slid off the brake pedal. Within seconds the rest of the posse followed the initial shots with a massive show of force. Dozens and dozens of bullets flew at the car and its two occupants (later counts of rounds fired ranged from a hundred and fifty to more than two hundred). Glass shattered, metal broke apart, bullets hit the tires. In the maelstrom of lead, the men in the posse later reported hearing Bonnie scream. It was a short one.

As the bullet-pocked car rolled to a stop, Hamer moved in

close to make sure of their work. He used his most powerful rifle to fire multiple shots at both now-lifeless bodies. One report says he even leaned into the smoking car and fired directly at Bonnie, who was clearly already dead.

Sixteen seconds, hundreds of bullets, two dead outlaws.

It was a gruesome scene, with both bodies perforated repeatedly and blood and body tissues spread in the car. Hinton filmed the aftermath, capturing the moment when Bonnie's body sprawled partway out of the car when her door was finally opened. In a move that would certainly not be condoned today, the lawmen helped themselves to the couple's possessions. Simmons had actually given Hamer permission to take Clyde's arsenal for himself. A suitcase of money that the Barrow family said Clyde had showed them was taken. Even Clyde's saxophone was carried away as the spoils of victory.

The bodies were left in the car as a tow truck came to haul the wrecked Ford V-8 back into town. A kind of parade came together, with the posse's cars joined by the tow truck, a coroner's car, and then by various onlookers eager to see the gruesome scene. Amazingly, as the parade moved through the town of Gibsland nearby, the tow truck broke down in front of an elementary school. Hundreds of children at recess swarmed around the car, even pulling off a bloody sheet to see the carnage for themselves. The news spread quickly, and the tiny town was soon overwhelmed with gawking visitors. People even tried to grab souvenirs, parts of the car or even parts of the bodies. One man was stopped from trying to pull a ring from Clyde's finger. Shockingly, photos taken of the dead bodies, both clothed and naked, were released to the press, which printed them gleefully.

In another move that would horrify people today, Hamer let locals walk through the coroner's office to view the bodies in person. The official story was to show people the wages of sin, as Bonnie had written. But probably it was just because so many people were morbidly curious.

By the next day some order had been restored. Henry Barrow arrived to escort his son's body back home. Bonnie's body was sent back to Dallas too. They were sent to separate funeral homes. Their wish to be buried together would not be fulfilled.

Back in Dallas the public mania for the dead couple continued and even grew. The day after the shooting, the two funeral homes opened for public visitation. This was a practice typically done for family and friends, not for the general public. It was a huge mistake, as more than ten thousand people lined up at each home to walk past the corpses of the legendary outlaws. Police had to be called to both places to keep order. Film of the event shows many people dressed in their finest clothes, smiling and laughing as they took part in this grim ritual.

Clyde was buried on that Friday, next to his brother Buck.

Bonnie was buried in another cemetery, attended by the Barrow family along with the Parkers. In a now-stunning display of bad taste, local Dallas newspapers sent a huge batch of flowers in thanks to the couple for helping them sell so many papers.

~ 22 ~

FOLK HEROES

The violent deaths of Bonnie and Clyde kicked off a summer of gunfire in America. Law enforcement, including the newly empowered FBI, caught or killed Dillinger, Floyd, Baby Face Nelson, and Ma and Fred Barker in the coming months. New laws were passed that gave federal authorities much greater power in combating criminals who crossed state lines. Just robbing a bank became a federal crime, regardless of state lines, a law that remains in force today. Police also began creating wide radio networks, the better to coordinate among themselves.

Bonnie and Clyde "memorabilia" became a growing business. Hamer sold off the guns he had taken from the car (even refusing a plea from Cumie Barrow to return them to the family). The vehicle itself, after a court case, was returned to the Kansas family from which it was stolen. They then rented it to a man who put it on a truck that toured the country showing off the "death car."[76] A year later, in need of money, Cumie Barrow and other Barrows, along with Emma Parker, joined the national tour of the death car, giving speeches and answering questions in front of paying crowds about the gruesome deaths of their children.

The car in which Bonnie and Clyde were killed is now on view at a casino in Primm, Nevada.

Marie Barrow sold a stash of Clyde's things in the 1990s, including the clothing he wore when killed and some of his remaining weapons. Even now, curiosity seekers can find pieces from the couple's lives for sale at auction houses and from collectors.

Henry Methvin did get his pardon from Texas, but he was later convicted of killing Cal Campbell in Oklahoma and served eight years. Joe Palmer and Raymond Hamilton were captured in 1934 and died in the electric chair in 1935 for their part in several murders.

W. D. Jones also met a violent end, but not until 1974, when he was shot by the boyfriend of a woman he had just met.

As for Bonnie and Clyde, the public continued to be fascinated by a couple in love and in constant trouble. *Fugitives* was the first book on them, though both the Barrow and Parker families later said that their co-author, Jan Fortune, made up a lot of what was in the book. Members of both families later worked with other authors on their own versions of Bonnie and Clyde, versions that often clashed or left out large chunks of information. Fiction writers used the couple as the models for a wide range of gangland stories, further confusing the real couple with the made-up ones.

Several movies were made in the late 1930s and 1940s that were inspired by the couple and the Barrow gang. Bonnie and Clyde's personalities varied from film to film, but none purported to be completely true anyway.

By the late 1950s, the American entertainment landscape had found many new outlets for its curiosity, and the outlaw era faded from view. Then in 1967 Bonnie and Clyde got new life in the public eye. Actor and director Warren Beatty starred in a movie he helped produce about the couple. It won several awards and was notable for the bloody and violent depiction of the couple's deaths. Beatty and costar Faye Dunaway were covered with "squibs" filled with fake blood. As they danced and jerked and flung themselves about, the squibs exploded over and over, covering their clothes with blood. Unlike in real life, the couple was shown exiting the car during the shooting. Relatives and historians quibbled with other parts of the film, but regardless of its accuracy, the movie cemented the outlaw couple as parts of American legend.

Though most of the references to them had for decades been about Clyde and Bonnie or the Barrow gang, Beatty's film was called *Bonnie & Clyde*. That's how they've been ever since, together in death as they were in life.

This is the most famous of Bonnie's poems. In it she recalls some of her adventures with Clyde, but pointedly notes some things of which they were accused that they did not do. For people who clearly did some awful things, they were very sensitive about such false accusations. They call out the police for pinning just about any crime, especially in Dallas, on the pair. But amid that, she realizes the eventual futility of their chosen life and correctly predicts their end.

THE STORY OF BONNIE AND CLYDE
OR "THE END OF THE LINE"

You've read the story of Jesse James

Of how he lived and died;

If you're still in need

Of something to read,

Here's the story of Bonnie and Clyde.

Now Bonnie and Clyde are the Barrow gang,

I'm sure you all have read

How they rob and steal

And those who squeal

Are usually found dying or dead.

There's lots of untruths to these write-ups;

They're not so ruthless as that;

Their nature is raw;

They hate all the law

The stool pigeons, spotters, and rats.

They call them cold-blooded killers;

They say they are heartless and mean;

But I say this with pride,

That I once knew Clyde

When he was honest and upright and clean.

But the laws fooled around,

Kept taking him down

And locking him up in a cell,

Till he said to me,

"I'll never be free,

So I'll meet a few of them in hell."

The road was so dimly lighted;

There were no highway signs to guide;

But they made up their minds

If all roads were blind,

They wouldn't give up till they died.

The road gets dimmer and dimmer;

Sometimes you can hardly see;

But it's fight, man to man,

And do all you can,

For they know they can never be free.

From heart-break some people have suffered;

From weariness some people have died;

But take it all in all,

Our troubles are small

Till we get like Bonnie and Clyde.

If a policeman is killed in Dallas,

And they have no clue or guide;

If they can't find a fiend,

They just wipe their slate clean

And hang it on Bonnie and Clyde.

There's two crimes committed in America

Not accredited to the Barrow mob;

They had no hand

In the kidnap demand,

Nor the Kansas City depot job.

A newsboy once said to his buddy;

"I wish old Clyde would get jumped;

In these awful hard times

We'd make a few dimes

If five or six cops would get bumped."

The police haven't got the report yet,

But Clyde called me up today;

He said, "Don't start any fights

We aren't working nights

We're joining the NRA."

From Irving to West Dallas viaduct

Is known as the Great Divide,

Where the women are kin,

And the men are men,

And they won't "stool" on Bonnie and Clyde.

If they try to act like citizens

And rent them a nice little flat,

About the third night

They're invited to fight

By a sub-gun's rat-tat-tat.

They don't think they're too tough or desperate,

They know that the law always wins;

They've been shot at before,

But they do not ignore

That death is the wages of sin.

Some day they'll go down together;

And they'll bury them side by side;

To few it'll be grief

To the law a relief

But it's death for Bonnie and Clyde.

—Bonnie Parker

NOTES

1. Jan I. Fortune, *Fugitives: The Story of Clyde Barrow and Bonnie Parker* (Dallas: Ranger Press, Inc., 1937), Kindle edition, chapter 1.
2. Jeff Guinn, *Go Down Together: The True, Untold Story of Bonnie and Clyde* (New York: Simon & Schuster, 2009), Kindle edition, chapter 1.
3. James R. Knight, *Bonnie and Clyde: A Twenty-First Century Update* (Forth Worth, TX: Eakin Press, 2003), Kindle edition, chapter 2.
4. Fortune, *Fugitives*, ch. 1.
5. Guinn, *Go Down Together*, ch. 4.
6. Fortune, *Fugitives*, ch. 2.
7. Fortune, *Fugitives*, ch. 3.
8. Fortune, *Fugitives*, ch. 3.
9. Knight, *Bonnie and Clyde*, ch. 5.
10. Guinn, *Go Down Together*, ch. 4.
11. Guinn, *Go Down Together*, ch. 4.
12. Guinn, *Go Down Together*, ch. 4.
13. Guinn, *Go Down Together*, ch. 4.
14. A&E documentary, *Bonnie & Clyde*, 2013.
15. Guinn, *Go Down Together*, ch. 5.
16. Guinn, *Go Down Together*, ch. 5.
17. Guinn, *Go Down Together*, ch. 5.
18. Guinn, *Go Down Together*, ch. 5.
19. Guinn, *Go Down Together*, ch. 5.
20. Guinn, *Go Down Together*, ch. 5.
21. Guinn, *Go Down Together*, ch. 5.
22. Fortune, *Fugitives*, ch. 4.
23. Knight, *Bonnie and Clyde*, ch. 11.
24. Fortune, *Fugitives*, ch. 7.
25. Guinn, *Go Down Together*, ch. 6.
26. Guinn, *Go Down Together*, ch. 6.
27. John Neal Phillips, *Running with Bonnie and Clyde: The Ten Fast Years of Ralph Fults* (Norman, OK: University of Oklahoma Press, 2002), Kindle edition, chapter 6.
28. Fortune, *Fugitives*, ch. 7.
29. Phillips, *Running with Bonnie and Clyde*, preface.
30. A&E documentary, *Bonnie & Clyde*.

31. Fortune, *Fugitives*, ch 8.

32. Fortune, *Fugitives*, ch. 8.

33. Guinn, *Go Down Together*, ch. 9.

34. Fortune, *Fugitives*, ch. 10.

35. Guinn, *Go Down Together*, ch. 10.

36. W. D. Jones, "Riding with Bonnie and Clyde," *Playboy*, November (1968).

37. Jones, "Riding with Bonnie and Clyde."

38. Jones, "Riding with Bonnie and Clyde."

39. Guinn, *Go Down Together*, ch. 15.

40. Fortune, *Fugitives*, ch .13.

41. Jones, "Riding with Bonnie and Clyde."

42. Fortune, *Fugitives*, ch. 13.

43. Guinn, *Go Down Together*, ch. 22.

44. Jones, "Riding with Bonnie and Clyde."

45. Jones, "Riding with Bonnie and Clyde."

46. Fortune, *Fugitives*, ch. 13.

47. Guinn, *Go Down Together*, ch. 19.

48. Guinn, *Go Down Together*, ch. 19.

49. Jones, "Riding with Bonnie and Clyde."

50. Guinn, *Go Down Together*, ch. 19.

51. Jones, "Riding with Bonnie and Clyde."

52. Guinn, *Go Down Together*, ch. 22, and Fortune, *Fugitives,* ch. 13.

53. Portal to Texas History, Jones statement (11-18-33), https://texashistory.unt.edu.

54. Guinn, *Go Down Together*, ch. 22.

55. Guinn, *Go Down Together*, ch. 22.

56. Phillips, *Running with Bonnie and Clyde*, 160.

57. Guinn, *Go Down Together*, ch. 23.

58. Knight, *Bonnie and Clyde,* ch. 29.

59. Knight, *Bonnie and Clyde,* ch. 29.

60. Nate Hendley, *Bonnie and Clyde: A Biography*, (Westport, CT: Greenwood Press 2007), Kindle edition, chapter 7.

61. Phillips, *Running with Bonnie and Clyde*, 172.

62. *Time*, March 11 (1935).

63. Guinn, *Go Down Together*, ch. 23.

64. Jim Wilson, "Frank Hamer, Legendary Lawman," https://www.americanrifleman.org/articles/2011/9/22/frank-hamer-legendary-lawman.

65. Knight, *Bonnie and Clyde*, ch. 31.

66. Guinn, *Go Down Together*, ch. 28.

67. Knight, *Bonnie and Clyde*, ch. 32.

68. Guinn, *Go Down Together*, prologue.

69. Guinn, *Go Down Together*, prologue.

70. Knight, *Bonnie and Clyde*, ch. 32.

71. Guinn, *Go Down Together*, ch. 28.

72. Knight, *Bonnie and Clyde*, ch. 33.

73. Knight, *Bonnie and Clyde*, ch. 34.

74. Fortune, *Fugitives*, ch. 13.

75. Guinn, *Go Down Together*, ch. 37.

76. Guinn, *Go Down Together*, afterword.

SOURCES

Bonnie and Clyde: American Experience. Video produced in 2016 for PBS. http://www.pbs.org/wgbh/americanexperience/films/bonnieclyde.

FBI website about the couple: https://www.fbi.gov/history/famous-cases /bonnie-and-clyde.

Fortune, Jan I. *Fugitives: The Story of Clyde Barrow and Bonnie Parker.* Dallas: Ranger Press, Inc., 1937.

Guinn, Jeff. *Go Down Together: The True, Untold Story of Bonnie and Clyde.* New York: Simon & Schuster, 2009.

Hendley, Nate. *Bonnie and Clyde: A Biography.* Westport, CT: Greenwood Press, 2007.

Jones, W. D. "Riding with Bonnie and Clyde." *Playboy.* November, 1968.

Knight, James R. *Bonnie and Clyde: A Twenty-First Century Update.* Forth Worth, TX: Eakin Press, 2003.

Phillips, John Neal. *Running with Bonnie and Clyde: The Ten Fast Years of Ralph Fults.* Norman, OK: University of Oklahoma Press, 2002.

Wilson, Jim. "Frank Hamer, Legendary Lawman." https://www .americanrifleman.org/articles/2011/9/22/frank-hamer-legendary-lawman.

ABOUT THE AUTHOR

James Buckley Jr. is a prolific author of nonfiction for young readers. *Bonnie and Clyde* is his second book in the History's Worst series, following *Adolf Hitler*. Both of those books join a long list of biographies that includes Milton Hershey, Betsy Ross, Jesse Owens, Muhammad Ali, and Roberto Clemente, among many others. His other recent books are titles about the International Space Station, the moon, snakes, insects, firefighters, history, and sports. That last subject is a big part of his work, following a career in sports journalism with *Sports Illustrated* and the National Football League. He is the owner of Shoreline Publishing Group, a book packager in Santa Barbara, California, where he lives with his wife and two teenagers.